The Castles of Herefordshire.

Cowells Anastatic Press, Ipswich.

A

HISTORY

OF THE

AND

THEIR LORDS

BY THE

REV. CHARLES J. ROBINSON, M.A.

VICAR OF NORTON CANON AND CHAPLAIN TO THE EARL OF CAITHNESS.

LOGASTON PRESS
Little Logaston, Logaston,
Woonton, Almeley, Herefordshire HR3 6QH

First published by Logaston Press 2002

ISBN 1 873827 68 7

Printed in Great Britain by
Antony Rowe Ltd

To the Venerable the Right Honourable

Frederick Twistleton Wykeham Fiennes,

D.C.L.,

THIRTEENTH BARON SAYE AND SELE,

ARCHDEACON OF HEREFORD,

&c., &c.,

This Volume is Dedicated in Grateful Acknowledgment of many

Kindnesses and much Encouragement.

PREFACE.

SIR WALTER SCOTT was one of the first persons to detect, perhaps because he shared so largely in it, that latent taste for antiquarian pursuits which exists in the minds of most Englishmen. He says, truly enough, that the mere attribute of antiquity in an object is sufficient to call forth vivid feelings and lively associations. The relic itself may possess no grandeur of size, little grace and less utility, yet if it be "even the rudest remnant of a feudal tower, even the obscure and almost undistinguishable vestige of an altogether unknown edifice, it has power to awaken trains of fancy and kindle in us a fellow-feeling with the "son of the winged days" over whose fallen habitation we pass." * Scott himself had these inborn feelings highly developed by the circumstances with which he was surrounded. His childish ears were familiar with the ballads of the Northern border; his youthful imagination was fed with the tales and traditions which cling around its ruined castles and desecrated shrines.

* *Remarks on the Poems of Patrick Carey.*

The Western Borderland is perhaps as rich in monuments of the past as the Northern, and abounds in spots about which we may say with truth,

> We never tread upon them but we set
> Our feet upon some reverend history. *

But the memorials are hard to decipher, and certainly the traditions live no longer upon the lips of men. The peasant ploughs with stolid unconcern the site of some ancient camp or field of blood; the shepherd folds his flock within some ruined castle, and each is as ignorant of the past associations of the place as the modern Mexican, who shares in the astonishment of the traveller at the fragments of giant temples on which he stumbles in his native forests.

The writer has no theory whereby to account for the unmerited neglect with which the relics of "Old Herefordshire" have hitherto been treated, but he indulges the hope that by means of the following pages he may be permitted to rescue one class of them from absolute oblivion and to help in preserving, if not their material fabrics, at least the historic memories of some of the Border Castles.

It should be observed that in the present work the word "Castle" has been employed in its popular sense, and is not intended to apply exclusively to the true Castle or Norman fortalice. It must be understood

---

* *Webster's Duchess of Malfy.*

to embrace all fortified mansions erected anterior to the union of the Houses of York and Lancaster to which the appellation of *Castra* has been given in documents. This limitation may seem arbitrary, but it has been rendered necessary by the fact that life and liberty were held on such insecure tenure in the Welsh Marches that every lord regarded his house as his Castle and invested it with many of the characteristics of the latter.*

It only remains for the writer to express his grateful thanks to the numerous friends and correspondents who have assisted him in the preparation of this volume, and especially to record his deep obligation to the Lady Frances Vernon Harcourt, whose faithful sketches give a value to his work which it would not otherwise possess, and evince the interest which the artist takes in the County with which her ancestors have been so long and so honourably connected.

---

* Should the writer meet with sufficient encouragement, he would be glad to devote his leisure to the preparation of a companion volume upon the old manor-houses of Herefordshire, their associations and the fortunes of the families that have dwelt within them.

Preface to this Edition

Following on from the reissue of the Reverend Charles Robinson's *A History of the Mansions & Manors of Herefordshire* in 2001, the Herefordshire Family History Society, amongst others, have requested that we do the same for this volume. The book has therefore been repaginated and reindexed along similar lines to those adopted in the reissue of *Mansions & Manors,* and once again thanks are due to John Wilson for his work on the index. The overall size of this volume has been slightly reduced from the original so that the two 'Logaston Press' volumes make a complementary pair.

Reverend Charles J. Robinson was vicar of Norton Canon and president of the Woolhope Naturalists' Field Club in 1875. *A History of the Castles of Herefordshire and Their Lords* was first published in 1869, since when many books and papers have appeared that take our knowledge further. One of the more recent was Ron Shoesmith's *Castles and Moated Sites of Herefordshire*. Although currently out of print, it is hoped to bring out a further edition in the not too distant future.

Andy Johnson and Ron Shoesmith
Logaston Press
August 2002

Brampton Brian 1841

CONTENTS

Almeley Castle.

◆•◆

UPON the edge of a rivulet beside the Church of Almeley is a grass-grown mound, upon which the keep of an ancient Castle formerly stood. The name, Old Castle, was till lately attached to the farm, (now called Old Court) which occupies the site of the fortress; and no doubt the moat, which encircled the latter and formed its chief defence, was fed by the brook, on which the lapse of centuries has had no effect.

We have no evidence as to the age in which Almeley Castle was built. The termination, *ley*, indicates that the forest had been sufficiently cleared to allow cattle to be depastured there, and there are some faint indications of its having been occupied as a Roman encampment. But neither in the Domesday Survey, nor in the earliest lists of Border fortifications, do we find any notice of the existence of a Castle at Almeley. We may, however, hazard the conjecture that the Oldcastles, who were its occupants throughout the fourteenth century, derived their name in the first instance from the fact that they dwelt on the site of the Roman camp, and afterwards, by a very natural process, attached that name permanently to the fortified building which they there erected.

Though not a vestige of the Castle now remains, yet its ruins were visible in the middle of the seventeenth century, and a tradition is still current that Sir John Oldcastle, the Lollard Martyr, (better known as Lord Cobham) had once lived within its walls. *(Harl. MSS. 6726 and 6868.)*

This tradition is confirmed by abundant evidence, and we may venture to assert that Almeley has a much better claim to be considered the Martyr's birth-place than the remote village of Oldcastle which stands on the right bank of the Monnow, beyond the limits of Herefordshire. It is at any rate certain that in 1368 John de Oldcastle, Lord Cobham's grandfather, presented to the living of Almeley, (*Reg. Charlton*) and that either he, or his son Thomas who was Sheriff of Herefordshire in 1386 and 1391, granted the advowson to the Priory of Wormesley.

Sir John Oldcastle (Lord Cobham in right of his wife) was born about the year 1360, and served the office of Sheriff of his native county in the seventh year of Henry IV. As a wit, a poet, and a soldier, he gained some distinction in his younger days, but his claim to celebrity rests mainly upon the courage and consistency he displayed in supporting the doctrines of Wickliffe and the cause of Ecclesiastical Reform. To his great local influence was due the rapid spread of Lollardism throughout Herefordshire, and it was thither that he fled for shelter when his overt acts of treason had roused the anger of his *quondam* boon companion, Henry V. He was arrested at Broniarth, in the parish of Guilsfield, Montgomeryshire, conveyed to London, and on Christmas day, 1417, burnt alive as a traitor and a heretic, leaving behind him a reputation peculiarly ambiguous. The evidence as to his character which has come down to us, is so conflicting that it is almost impossible to arrive at a distinct conclusion. Even from the stage, where the popular opinion of a man is generally expressed in plain terms, no certain verdict can be obtained. Shakspeare held him up to ridicule as a profligate buffoon, under the character of Sir John Falstaffe, " my old lad of the Castle ;" but on the other hand, dramatists of almost equal popularity, and at the same date, represented the Lollard knight as a man of strong religious convictions, for which he was ready to sacrifice wealth, station, and even life itself. *(See " The True and Honourable History of the Life of Sir John Oldcastle." 1600. A drama ascribed to Munday, Drayton and others. And cf Bale. " A brefe chronycle concernynge the examynacyon and death of the blessed martyr of Christ, Syr Johan Oldecastell. Reprint 1729.)* The readiest, and perhaps the fairest, solution of the difficulty is to suppose that Falstaffe is a true representation of Oldcastle in his youth, and that the great popularity which Henry V achieved, and the re-action which set in after the temporary success of Lollardism combined to throw an undeserved shadow over the character of the man who, in his later years, became the king's opponent and the Reformer's stoutest champion.

By the attainder of Lord Cobham, Almeley and the other possessions of Oldcastle became confiscated to the Crown, though there is some ground to suppose that his son Henry obtained, in 1428, a restoration of part of the estates, *(see Appendix I)* and thus Almeley became soon afterwards the property of his heirs, the Milbournes. In the reign of Henry VII, one of the twelve co-heiresses of Sir Simon Milbourne, of Tillington, in the parish of Burghill, brought it in dower to Thomas Monnington, of Sarnesfield, whose descendants possessed it in 1670. *(Blount's MS.)*

From the Monningtons it passed to the Pembers of Newport and thence, again by purchase, to the Foleys of the same place. It is now the property of James Gibson Watt, Esq., of Newport House, having been bought by him a few years ago from R. Foley Onslow, Esq.

Ashperton

ADJOINS the little parish of Stretton Gransham or Grandison and with it formed part of the possessions of a feudal family of the latter name in the thirteenth century.

William de Grandison, the son of a Burgundian noble, (the ruins of whose castle on the lake of Neuchatel are familiar to the Swiss tourist) obtained a grant of land in Herefordshire from Edward I and added largely to it by his marriage with the wealthy heiress of John de Tregoz *(See Eaton Tregoz)*. In the year 1292 he had license from the King "to crenellate his mansion at Asperton" and was summoned to Parliament from the 27th year of Edward I to the 19th year of Edward II inclusive. The date of his death is unknown, but Leland states that both he and his wife Sibil were buried at Dore Abbey. *(Leland Itin. VIII 84 b.)* Three of the children of William de Grandison achieved considerable distinction in their day. The best known of them, John de Grandison, is said to have been born at Ashperton, which was presumably the birth-place of his brothers also. *(Fuller's Worthies.)*

John de Grandison probably owed some of his success in life to his great-uncle Bishop Cantilupe, "St. Thomas of Hereford," or rather to his venerated memory. He was made Bishop of Exeter in 1327 and has been compared to the late occupant of that see in respect of the extraordinary duration of his episcopate (forty-two years), the extent of his acquirements, and what Fuller calls his "Stout Stomach," shewn especially in resisting Archbishop Meopham, *vi et armis*, when he came to visit his diocese. He founded the Collegiate Church of Ottery St. Mary in Devonshire and contributed largely to the embellishment of his own Cathedral. *(Worthies of England.)*

The bishop's elder brother Sir Peter was summoned to the first three Parliaments of Edward III and died in the 30th year of that reign. He lies buried in Hereford Cathedral and his monument, long supposed to commemorate one of the Bohuns, is a beautiful piece of sculpture and will be found on the north side of the Lady Chapel. Four of the figures with which it is enriched, viz. : St. Ethelbert, St. John the Baptist, and the two English St. Thomases, were recovered by Mr. Cottingham, the architect, from behind the choir-screen where they were concealed amidst rubbish and fragments of stone.

Sir Otho Grandison, a younger brother, was a statesman as well as a warrior and was sent by Edward II, in the first year of his reign, as ambassador to the Pope. He died in 1359 and in his will "entreats that no armed horse nor armed man be allowed to go before his body on his burial day, nor that his body be covered with any cloth painted in gilt or signed with his arms; but that it be only of white cloth marked with a cross." *(Nicolas Test. Vetusta.)*

The Castle of the Grandisons has wholly disappeared. The site on which it stood, now belonging to the Rev. John Hopton, was planted about the close of the last century, when the foundations were grubbed up, but the moat still exists and is full of water. Two hundred years ago the park (then belonging to the Lingens) was "well wooded but contained no deer." *(Harl. MS. 6726.)* It is now a coppice wood of more than a hundred acres in extent and forms part of the property of Lady Emily Foley.

Brampton Brian Castle.

— ◆·◉·◆ —

THE foundation of Brampton Brian Castle may with much probability be assigned to the later years of the reign of King Henry I. Barnard Unspec, Lord of Kinlet in Shropshire, seems to have been the first of his family to adopt the designation "de Brampton," and we may therefore conjecture that he made the latter place his usual residence and erected there some sort of fortified dwelling upon the low land which favoured the construction of a moat. In 1179 we find his grandson Brian de Brampton associated with Sir Hugh de Mortimer in establishing the neighbouring Abbey of Wigmore. He laid the second stone of the foundation and granted materials for the work from his woods and quarries. His son, husband of Matilda de Braose, a member of the most powerful family in the Welsh Marches, added the advowson of the Church of Kinlet to the endowment of the Abbey. Their descendants remained at Brampton for four generations, when the line terminated in two co-heirs, the elder of whom married Robert de Harley, (called by Roger de Mortimer "his beloved Bachelor,") and carried the Castle and manor into that family. At an inquest held in 1293 after the death of the last Bryan de Brampton the Castle was described as a Tower with curtilage, garden and vivary, valued at £8 7s. 8d. per annum, and held under the Mortimers by the performance of Castle guard at Wigmore for forty days in war-time and by a yearly rent of 13s. 4d. *(Inq. p. m., 23 Edw. I.)*

Bryan, the second son of Robert de Harley, succeeded to his mother's property in the County of Hereford and both he and his son were

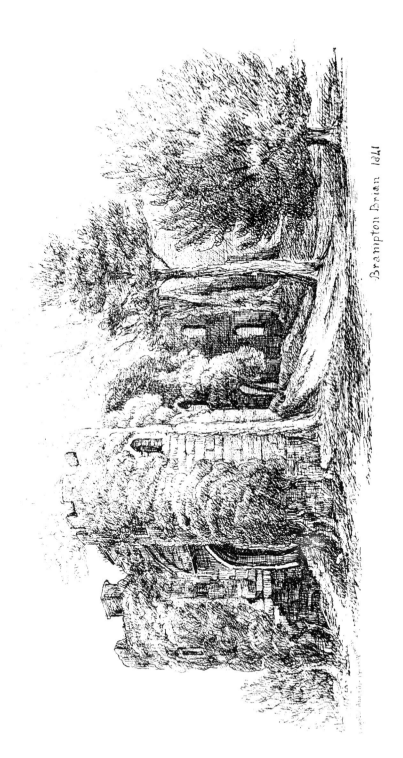

Brampton Brian 1841

conspicuous for their martial enterprise. The former, in recognition of his valour, was named by the Black Prince for the honour of the Garter, and the latter was permitted to substitute for the usual cognizance of the family the suggestive crest of a demi-lion issuing from a tower of three turrets. It is to one or other of these warriors that we should ascribe the building of the gateway of Brampton Castle. It is the most ancient part of the existing remains and in one or two places above the archway and windows, may be traced the ball-flower, characteristic of the Edwardian era.

In the Wars of the Roses the Harleys took the field under the banner of the House of York, with which they were connected by ties of blood as well as by the friendship of generations. On the walls of the old hall at Brampton there doubtless once shone the spurs of knighthood won by John Harley at Tewkesbury, and the trusty sword which his grandson wielded at Flodden Field.

The Castle concealed for some time the celebrated Jesuits, Parsons and Campion, when upon their secret tour through England in 1580, and great hopes were indulged that they would obtain the same ascendancy over their patron's son which they had secured over his father. Their failure marks, perhaps, the commencement of that tendency towards Puritanism which had its full development in the next generation. Sir Robert Harley, who succeeded to Brampton at the death of his father in 1631, was one of the few persons of distinction in Herefordshire who took the side of the Parliament in the great constitutional struggle of the seventeenth century. A more temporizing policy than that which he displayed at its outset might probably have helped to preserve his fortune, but it would also have deprived the Castle of the chief historic interest which attaches to it, and prevented a display of heroism which added a new lustre to the name of Harley.

Sir Robert was compelled by his duties as Member of Parliament for the County to reside in London. The custody of the Castle was, therefore, entrusted to his wife Brilliana, who, though willing to leave to others the decision whether it would be "beest to goo away from Brampton or by God's healp to stand it out," had no fear of the result of any contest. Her own was also "God's cause in which it would be an honour to suffer," though she herself was well assured "that the Lord would show the men of the world that it is hard fighting against heaven." *(Lady Harley's Letters, Vol. LVIII, Camden Soc. Pub.)*

Throughout the critical years 1642 and 1643, when the tide of fortune had not set distinctly in either direction, Lady Harley had to feel the anxious isolation of her position. Scarcely one county family besides the Kyrles and Westphalings had joined the side of the Parliament, while among the King's staunchest adherents were Coningsby, Scudamore, Croft, Lingen, and Pye, who might well be supposed to carry all Herefordshire with them.

The very indecision of her enemies harassed her. For more than twelve months before the actual siege commenced there had been threats that Brampton would be assailed. In the winter of 1642 the rumours became more coherent — the farms were to be burnt and the Castle blockaded. Later on a council of war decided that "the best way to take Brampton was to blow it up." On Valentine's day 1643 Lady Brilliana writes "The Sheriff of Radnorshire with the trained bands of that county and some of the Hearfordsheare soulders mean to come against me. My Lord Harberd had appointed a day to come to Prestine that so his presence might perswade them to goo out of theire county. He had commanded them to bringe pay for vitals for 10 days. The soulders came to Prestine but it pleased God to call my Lord Harberd another way. . . . Now they say they will starve me out of my howes. They have taken away all your Father's rents and now they will drive away the cattell and then I shall have nothing to live upon, for all theire ame is to enfors me to let the men I have goo, that then they might seese upon my howes and cute our throughts by a feewe Rooges and then say they knowe not whoo did it." She further adds, "they have used all means to have me leave no man in my howes and tell me I should be safe, but I have no caus to trust them." Her own mind was now made up to hold the Castle at any hazard. No time was lost in collecting stores and putting the building into an efficient state of repair. The lead was recast, the timber renewed and money borrowed from a friendly neighbour for the costly work of re-filling the moat. The little garrison was further strengthened by the addition of a serjeant from Col. Massie's division, "a brave and abell souldier" who had served in the German wars. This veteran (whose name, Hackluyt, recalls the adventurous spirit of a former generation) took the command of the retainers, mounted the guns and, together with Dr. Nathan Wright, the family physician, converted the mansion once more into a "small yet strong castle." *(Silas Taylor's MS. Harl. MS. 6726.)*

As the crisis drew near, the spirit of its gallant but delicate mistress rose and her letters to her son became more and more cheerful. At the end of June she was able to say, " I thank God I doo beyond my expectations or that of some in my house : my provitions heald out and I have borrowed yet not much money." On the 26th of the following month Sir Wm. Vavasour sat down before the Castle with a force of six hundred men, but nothing had been done towards reducing it by the 22nd of August, when he was summoned to Gloucester to sustain the falling fortunes of the King. He entrusted the command to Colonel Lingen, a Herefordshire man, who united zeal for his sovereign with a special animosity against a recreant neighbour. The inmates of the Castle were full of courage and sustained the attacks of the insurgents with unfailing gallantry. The old Register at Brampton states that the Church and town were burnt during the siege, but there is nothing to shew that the Castle sustained any serious damage, or that there was much loss of life among its defenders.* Col. Lingen had to withdraw his baffled troops on the 6th of September when authentic news of the Royal disaster at Gloucester reached him.

---

* A MS. life of Mr. Pierson, Rector of Brampton, mentions that "the Cook in the Castle was shot by a poisoned bullett which murdered him with great torment and poysomness to the whole family. Also a running spring that furnished the town was poisoned at the Fountaine." *(Harl. MS. 7516.)*

C

Lady Brilliana did not long survive her triumph; the anxieties of the siege had undermined her health. Writing to her son on the 9th of October she tells him of her failing strength—of rumours of a fresh attack to be made on the Castle—of her own sure confidence that the Lord would deliver her. Her trust was fulfilled, for she died upon the day following the date of her letter.

Early in the spring of 1644 a fresh force under the command of Sir Michael Woodhouse, a stern and able officer who had just taken Hopton Castle, attacked the Castle with the superior skill that comes from lengthened practice. The defence by Dr. Wright and some seventy men was as gallant as before, but the walls could not stand before the artillery of the new assailants, and, when the outworks had fallen, the garrison was compelled to surrender at mercy. A contemporary authority tells us that the walls were battered even with the ground, leaving little else but the cellars. *(Harl. MS. 6726.)* The prisoners included the doctor and serjeant and also Sir Robert Harley's three younger children. We recognise the former under the titles of " Lieut-Coll. Wright and Capt. Hackluit " in whose behalf Sir Robert writes to Lord Denbigh in January 1645, requesting his Lordship's permission " to represent a part of his distress in the captivity of his poor children and friends taken at his house, Brampton Castle, most of them as he understands in Shrewsbury in prison." *(Denbigh MS. I, 190.)* Whether his intercession proved available does not appear; indeed the tide of circumstances soon rendered it superfluous. As the new year advanced the Royal cause declined, and before its last month expired Naseby had been lost and Hereford itself was in the hands of the Parliament.

So soon as the Commonwealth was established, it was placed within Sir Robert Harley's power to exact a recompense for the losses he had sustained. His steward's statement of them was as follows :

" A Particular of what loss my master Sir Robert Harley hath sustained by the enemy in the county of Hereford since these wars :—

	£	s.	d.
The stock of Cattle of all sorts - - - - - -	940	00	00
The loss of £1500 per ann: for 3 years - - - -	4500	00	00
The Castle itself being utterly ruined - - - -	3000	00	00
All the rich furniture and household goods belonging to the Castle - - - - - - -	2500	00	00
Two mills with Brewhouses and stables and other outhouses together with corn and hay valued at - - - - - - - - - - - -	950	00	00
A study of Books* valued at - - - - - -	200	00	00
Two parks† wholly laid open and destroyed - -	500	00	00
Timber and other wood cut down and destroyed,	300	00	00
Destroyed at least 500 deer - - - - - - -			
Destroyed more in corn at least - - - - -	100	00	00
	£12,990	00	00

This was brought to Westminster by Wm. Bayley the 23rd of July, 1646."

Parliament authorized him to levy a large portion of the amount upon the confiscated estate of Sir Henry Lingen, his *quondam* assailant. The Royalist Colonel was either absent or in prison when the order was given, and accordingly Edward Harley, Sir Robert's son, waited upon his wife‡

* This earlier Harleian collection is set down at a very modest valuation, for there is reason to believe that it comprised an invaluable store of historical documents. Dr. Bentley in the Dedication of his Horace to the Earl of Oxford (1713) terms it "Bibliotheca Locupletissima."

† This would seem to mean Brampton and Wigmore Parks, for Deerfold had been disparked at an earlier period.

‡ Collins (Peerage sub voce) and others erroneously call her the *widow* of Sir Henry Lingen, but Sir Robert Harley predeceased Col. Lingen by several years, and the story is related without this error by Auditor Harley in his MS. account of his father.

with an account of the property assigned to him, and enquired whether the particulars had been correctly set down and signed by her husband. On receiving her answer he returned the schedule, waiving all right or title to the estates which it had conferred upon him. A revenge so noble elevates the son to a level with his heroic mother. Her courage baffled her enemies : his forgiveness subdued them.

The existing remains of Brampton Brian Castle shew no traces of the Tower which formed the original edifice, and we can only conjecture that it might have stood upon the north-western side, where some fragments of an old wall, with doorway and windows, may still be seen close to the cellar of the Hall. As has been already stated, the earliest portion of the present ruins is the entrance gateway, which was probably built in the reign of Edward III. It is defended on either side by a low circular tower, pierced with loopholes on the ground-floor and surmounted by a crenellated parapet. A pointed arch of good proportions, the string-course above which is ornamented with trefoil ball-flowers, admits to a vaulted passage, in which a portcullis worked and cut off the approach to an inner doorway. Access to the towers is gained through narrow doorways, with ogee arches, opening into this passage which, at a distance of thirty feet from the entrance, terminates in two arches, almost circular, with a portcullis between them. " The architrave of the first of these arches has a quatrefoil ball-flower ornament. Thence to the doorway leading into the court is a distance of fifteen feet. This doorway has a pointed arch in coarse rubble-work. To the east of it is a small pointed doorway ; and there was a similar doorway, since altered, on the west. Two square-headed trefoil windows open out of the first floor above. On the opposite side of the court the hall was approached through a pointed arch by a flight of steps ; and on either side of the doorway are square-headed trefoil windows." (*Archæol. Cambrensis. 3rd S. vol. xiii. Paper by R. W. Banks, Esq.)*

The bay-windows in ashlar work with the depressed archway beneath them, which are very conspicuous in the engraving, are portions of the ornamental additions made to the interior of the court when the border fortress was converted into a domestic residence.   A rose appears upon one of the existing doorways, and we have no hesitation in assigning the erection of this part of the fabric to the middle of the sixteenth century. Leland, who visited it early in the reign of Henry VIII, speaks of Brampton as "a Pyle or Castle."   Perhaps from his use of the former term we may conclude that at that date the fortress chiefly consisted of the Pele tower, a strong and compact building of which numerous examples may still be seen upon the northern border, and that the Tudor additions had not then been made.

It is stated in Symond's Diary that the Castle was "pulled downe" by the Royalist forces, and in Pierson's Life that it was "utterly burnt," and though these statements do not quite agree with the account already extracted from Silas Taylor's contemporary MS., yet all authorities coincide in asserting that the ruin was complete. In this state it continued till the death of Sir Robert Harley as the following extract from a sermon preached at his funeral in 1657 testifies :

"When after the wars Sir Robert Harley returned into the country, and came to see what face Brampton look't, he rode towards his castle gate, and, seeing the ruins, put off his hat and said, 'God hath brought great desolation upon this place since I last saw it.   I desire to say 'The Lord hath given and the Lord hath taken away and blessed be the name of the Lord;' in his good time he will raise it up againe.   When His house is built, God (I trust) will build mine,' and observe that he took care to build this house or place of worship, and let his own lie buried still in its woeful ruins."   The preacher, the Rev. Thomas Froysell, Vicar of Clun, who was a kinsman of Sir Robert, concludes with a wish that was speedily fulfilled — "the Lord repair the Ruines of this Castle and build up this great Family."   Sir Edward Harley, on resigning the Governorship of Dunkirk in 1661, returned at once to his native country and shortly afterwards commenced building what is now called the Hall. As it stood partly upon the old site the new building was at first styled the Castle and retained that name till the eighteenth century.   It was used as a place of residence by Sir Edward Harley in 1665* and a few years later he commences a retrospect of his life with the words, " I was born at Brampton Castle October 21, 1624 ; I am now through divine long-suffering at Brampton Brian Oct. 21, 1673, forty-nine years old . . . . . This place which was justly waste and for divers years as the Region of the Shadow of death for the sins and iniquities of my Forefathers . . . now is made to me a goodly Heritage." *(Family MS. penes Lady Frances V. Harcourt.)*

Some rooms over the inner gateway were inhabited till about the middle of the last century, but having been rendered unsafe by a violent storm were dismantled. The present front was added about the year 1748 on the marriage of Edward, fourth Earl of Oxford and is shewn in *Kennion's Border Views.*

The modern Castle is not without its memories. Here was born Edward Harley, Auditor of the Imprest, to whose piety and public spirit Herefordshire is largely indebted : here, too, the first and most illustrious of the Earls of Oxford and Mortimer died in 1724, carrying with him to the grave a reputation which, to use the phrase of Clarendon, " vituperare ne inimici quidem possunt, nisi ut simul laudent."

The Castle is now the property of Lady Langdale, the eldest daughter and coheiress of Edward Harley, fifth Earl of Oxford and Mortimer, and the direct descendant of Robert de Harley, its possessor five centuries ago.

* A letter from Sir Edward to Lord Chancellor Clarendon is extant dated in this year from Brampton Brian.

18

Bransill 1869

Bransill Castle

IN the parish of Eastnor is probably the most modern erection of its kind within the County and partook less of the character of a fortress than of a defensible palace, or castellated mansion.

Richard Beauchamp, Esquire, the son and heir of John, first Lord Beauchamp of Powyk and sometime High Treasurer to King Henry VI, obtained license in 1449 (and again in 1460) to enclose three hundred acres of land in Eastnor as a park and to crenellate his mansion. (*Lic. Crenell: Rot. Turr. 29 and 36, H. 6.*) At the death of Richard, second Lord Beauchamp, in 1496, without male issue, his estates were divided amongst his three daughters, one of whom married William Rede, Esq., of Lugwardine and brought Bransill Castle into her husband's family. Their occupation of it, however, was so disturbed by ghostly visitants that Mr. Gabriel Rede about the year 1600 thought it prudent to consult " Mr. Allen of Gloster Hall in Oxford who was famous for his advice in these matters." (*Coningsby's MS.*) Allen, who according to Antony à Wood was "the father of all learning and virtuous industry," was not unknown in Herefordshire where probably others besides the servants of Holm Lacy considered the watch that he carried to be his familiar spirit. (*See a quaint anecdote in "Letters from the Bodleian Library", 1813.*) By his advice a couple of Lord Beauchamp's bones were procured and taken to Bransill "which ever afterwards was quiet." These wonder-working bones, portions of the Vertebræ, were long regarded as Heir-looms in the Rede family and escaped the destruction in which the contents of the Castle were involved when it was burnt in the Civil wars. In the last century there was still to be seen at New Court in Lugwardine (the seat of the Redes) a box labelled "Lord Beauchamp's bones", but the tradition attaching to them had died out. *(Coningsby's MS.)*

The ruins of Bransill are in a deep glen below Midsummer Hill, a branch of the Malvern range, surrounded by tangled underwood and overgrown with dense masses of ivy. Buck's view, taken as early as 1731, shews that most of the outward walls and towers were then standing and from it, and the more correct drawing made by Kennion about forty years later, we can get a tolerably clear conception of the building. It was quadrangular, (each side being about forty yards long,) and at the corners were four octagonal towers, one of which alone was standing in 1779. The entrance was by a gateway on the western side and the castle was defended by two moats, twenty yards apart, which may still be easily traced. When Kennion visited it the area of the building was almost covered with trees and occupied as a warren, suggesting, with one slight alteration, the poet's words :

> " Thus the great Hall was wholly broken down,
> *And where the peer devised his country's good*
> The hedgehog underneath the plaintain bores,
> The rabbit fondles his own harmless face,
> The slow worm creeps and the thin weasel there
> Follows the mouse."

Bransill was purchased from the Rede family in the middle of the last century by Mr. Cocks of Castleditch and is now the property of Earl Somers, his descendant.

In adopting the spelling "Bransill" we have followed the Ordnance Survey, but the Castle is sometimes called Bronsill, Brantsill and Bromeshill, all of which are probably variations of the Cymric *bryn*, the English *brow* (or ridge), and the Scotch *brae*.

Bredwardine about 1650

Site of Bredwardine Castle 1869

Bredwardine Castle.

THE epithet which Longfellow applies to the Rhine is one which in bygone days must have been peculiarly appropriate to the river Wye. It was emphatically a "castled" stream; and perhaps the part of it which would best remind the traveller of its foreign rival would be where the fortress of Bredwardine, standing high upon the right bank and almost within sight of the towers of Moccas, Clifford, Eardisley, and Hay, commanded the ferry by which alone the river could be crossed. A pilgrim in the middle ages might have seen a further likeness between the two streams; for, with less opportunity for its gratification, there was the same love of plunder among the lords of the border Castles as among the more notorious "Robbers of the Rhine." In fact, the feudal Baron, whether in England or in the Rhenish Palatinate, throve upon pillage: without it the armed retainers who thronged his hall would have had too little vent for their energies, and but scanty means of subsistence. And certainly Bredwardine Castle was most aptly situated alike for levying black mail and defying retaliation. Its hungry garrison could without much difficulty feast their eyes upon the herds of oxen which were sent, even in early times, to fatten on the rich pastures of Letton — pastures which have been said to vie with the valley of the Nile in fertility — and we may be sure that no hoof which once had trod the Castle yard would be permitted to leave it again. *Vestigia nulla retrorsum.* What the eye had seen the tongue would taste. The fortress, well victualled, might have "laughed a siege to scorn." In front, at the foot of a steep escarpment, flowed a rapid river which it was impossible to cross except

by the ferry; and on the landward side a moat, broad and deep, formed
the defence, strong in itself and further strengthened by a wild and rugged
country which, thinly peopled with dependent vassals, stretched southward
and westward to the Black Mountains.

Of the ancient owners of the Castle we have very imperfect
information. The author of Waverley has indeed made the name of
Bredwardine as familiar to this generation as the reputation of the
"Profound Doctor," whom Chaucer commemorates, had made it to our
countrymen some four hundred years ago. But the Border fortress cannot
claim to have been the birth-place either of the mythic Laird of Tully-
Veolan or of his more substantial namesake, the learned yet simple
Archbishop of Canterbury. Fuller, however, states that the latter, though
born in Sussex of a family which had been settled there for three
generations, derived his name and remoter lineage from a Herefordshire
stock. We may, therefore, without much presumption conclude that he
was descended from John de Bradwardine to whom, according to Silas
Taylor, the manor was granted at the Norman conquest. One Hugh de
Bradwardyn, described as the son of Stephen Pons (see Clifford) is
recorded to have given to the newly-founded Abbey of Craswall the free
use of his ferry. (Duncumb's Hist. ii. 281.) The date of that grant seems
to have been the beginning of the thirteenth century, and, if we are to believe
Silas Taylor, (Harl. MS. 6726,) the donor must have been a descendant of
the possessor of the Castle immediately after the Norman Conquest. Either
by marriage (as the Visitation pedigrees assert) or by some other way, the
Castle had become the property of the Baskerville family as early as the
year 1227, (see Appendix ii,) but the manor belonged to the Earl of Hereford,
and in the following century was held by Hugh Lacy as his mesne-lord by the
service of one knight's fee to the Castle of Brecon. (Inq. p.m. 17. Edw. iii.)

Sir Walter Baskerville married Elizabeth Lacy and died seised of
both Castle and manor, but his son John having no issue the property
reverted to his daughter Margaret who married Robert Fouleshurst of a
Cheshire family (see Ormerod ii. 201). Their descendants, after matching
with the families of Venables and Burley, terminated ultimately in one

William Fouleshurst, who died without issue in the year 1439. Bredwardyn Castle and manor were then declared to be the property of Sir John Baskerville, as next of kin, he being the great-grandson of Richard, the brother of the above-named Sir Walter Baskerville. *(Appendix ii. Inq. p.m. Will. Fouleshurst.)*

The documents to which reference has been made throw considerable light upon the condition of the Castle, which, as it was termed "the Old Castle" as early as the reign of Henry III, we may perhaps infer was built at or soon after the Norman Conquest. Possibly it might have been one of the many fortresses that were erected during the wars of Stephen and Maud, and, being condemned as *castra adulterina*, were dismantled in the reign of either the second or third Henry. Certain it is that in the Inquisition of John, son of Walter Baskerville, chevialer, (taken Sept. 4, 1374,) it is styled "a toft with appurtenances called the Castel place," without mention of any fortified dwelling, and seventy years afterwards it is described as *a waste site* of no annual value whatever. *(Inq. Will. Fouleshurst.)*

In what way the ruined castle and chief manor left the family of Baskerville and came into that of Vaughan we have been unable to discover with any certainty. The passage quoted below from Silas Taylor's MS. clearly implies that there were two branches of the Vaughan family at Bredwardine, one of early and the other of late settlement, and this is in some measure confirmed by the pedigrees of Vaughan as given in the Heraldic Visitations and gathered from the title-deeds of the property. The earlier Vaughans were contemporary with the Baskervilles, and derived their interest in the place from the marriage of Walter Sais (*i.e.* the Saxon) son of Rhosser Vaughan of Lechryd, with one of the co-heirs of Sir Walter Bredwardine of Bredwardine. Their son Rhosser married Ann, daughter of Sir Walter Devereux (a landholder of Bredwardine) and had issue the hero of Agincourt, Sir Roger Vaughan.

Now in the chancel of the parish church (itself a curious epitome of architecture) are two very interesting monuments, which Silas Taylor absurdly describes as belonging to John de Bredwardine and his son-in-law,—the former being lord of the place at the Norman Conquest. A careful examination of them is hardly needed in order to discredit such a supposition.

The earlier and larger effigy, somewhat rudely carved out of the soft local sandstone, has been a good deal mutilated so that the figure, originally of gigantic proportions, has now been curtailed by a Procrustean process to much the same length as the life-sized later effigy. We are thus deprived of the additional evidence which the greaves and spurs would have given as to its date, but enough remains to enable us to say with confidence that it is not earlier than the middle of the fourteenth century. It represents a warrior clad in a tight-fitting jupon, beneath which is a hauberk of chain mail extending almost to the knees. A belt, ornamented with roses, encircles the hips and from it depends on the right side a dagger and on the left, a sword. The elbow pieces appear to be of disc shape, but the form of the gauntlets cannot be traced. The helmet is conical and without vizor, and the gorget of chain mail is attached to the bassinet by the earlier and simpler arrangement of staples and lace. The head of the figure rests upon a cushion, at each side of which a winged angel kneels, but neither crest nor plume is visible. We can only conjecture that the warrior represented is either Walter Baskerville who died 42 Edw. III, or Walter de Bredwardine, the grandfather of Sir Roger Vaughan. We incline to the latter surmise because it does not appear that the Baskervilles made this place their residence, but chiefly lived at Eardisley in this county or at Pickthorn, county Salop.

The later effigy in alabaster, is a very beautiful example of monumental art. The knight is represented as clad from head to foot in plate armour, the arms are crossed upon the breast, the hands elevated, and the head is defended by an open conical bassinet. A tilting helmet forms the pillow and suspended from the neck is the collar of SS. The latter distinctive marks enable us to identify the knight without much hesitation. The armour shows that its wearer lived at the end of the 14th or beginning of the 15th century and the collar makes the later date almost a matter of certainty. It was purely a Lancastrian badge, conferred only on active partisans and not in use before quite the end of the 14th century. We have therefore to find among those connected with Bredwardine at that particular time some warrior of sufficient distinction to have gained this peculiar honour and also to have gained it by his military services to the house of Lancaster. No one could better meet both these requirements than Sir Roger Vaughan of Bredwardine. His marriage with the daughter of Sir David Gam, Shakespeare's Fluellen, is itself proof enough that he wore the Red Rose next his heart, while his death at Agincourt not only confirms the proof, but afforded, in its circumstances, an occasion for some signal mark of royal favour. Now the popular story is that on the field of Agincourt King Henry in his effort to save the life of his brother, the Duke of Gloucester, was hard beset by eighteen French knights who had sworn to beat the crown from his head or to die in the attempt. Already a gem had been struck from the diadem when, says tradition, David Gam, Roger Vaughan, and another rushed forward and saved the life of the king at the expense of their own. Before expiring they received from the king's hand the honour of knighthood and had certainly earned by their heroic self-sacrifice the right to wear the Lancastrian ensign.

The descendants of Sir Roger Vaughan are styled in the Visitation pedigrees 'of Bredwardine' for many generations, but the eventual owner of the Castle derived from a younger line. Sir William Vaughan of Talgarth married Catharine Havard and left issue a son Watkin Vaughan who married Janet, one of the co-heirs of Milo ap Harry. Bredwardine, the father's property, descended to the eldest son Henry Vaughan* (who married a daughter of James Boyle of Hereford by a daughter of Hugh Lewis of

---

* Rowland Vaughan, the second son, inherited from his mother New Court in the Golden Valley and was author of a curious work on irrigation entitled "Most approved and long experienced Water-workes &c., as also demonstration of a Project for the great benefit of the *Common-wealth* generally, but of *Herefordshire* especially. By Rowland Vaughan Esquire, London, 1610."

Harpton), and by his son Roger Vaughan Esq., the Castle was rebuilt and probably much of the old material employed in its construction. Our engraving represents this mansion and is copied from a sketch in the possession of Sir George Cornewall, Bart.

Silas Taylor's account to which we have already referred is as follows :— " The dwelling-house very fairly built by Roger Vaughan Esq. about the years 1639—1640 was an ancient and strong castle, retaining that title still. It was called anciently the Castle of Gronw, and the lands and tenements thereabouts belonging to it is still called by the name of the manor of Gronw. Another lordship in the parish belonging to the Vaughans is called the manor of Radnor, where near the house (which both anciently belonged unto and yet retains the name of the Court of the Vaughans, viz.—Sir George Vaughan, was sold to these Vaughans of Bredwardine about the year 1630.) There is a small fortified hill for the safeguard of the near inhabitants against any sudden inroad." *(Harl. MS. 6726.)*

It only remains to add that Roger Vaughan married Jone Husbands of Wormbridge (the family from which Mr. Clive derives that property) and left a son Henry Vaughan of Moccas and Bredwardine, whose widow married Edward Cornewall and conveyed both estates into the family of her second husband, the ancestor of Sir George Cornewall, Bt., to whom Bredwardine now belongs (*See Moccas.*)

Clifford

Cowslip Assidue Prae:Ipswich.

Clifford Castle.

⚜ ——●◆●—— ⚜

THE situation of Clifford, standing high upon the right bank of the river Wye and commanding the stream at a point where it is shallow enough for passage, not merely suggested its name but marked it from the earliest times as a suitable site for a border fortress.

Clifford is one of the five Herefordshire Castles mentioned in the Domesday Survey (A. D. 1086), being then in possession of Ralph de Todeni. It had been built, or more probably repaired, by William Fitz Osborne, Earl of Hereford, to whom it was granted at the Conquest by his relative William of Normandy. The Earl was slain in Flanders in 1070 and was succeeded by his youngest son Roger, surnamed de Bretevil, who conspired against his king in 1078 and, failing in his object, suffered imprisonment and the confiscation of his estates. Clifford was then granted to Ralph de Todeni (who was nearly allied to the Fitz-Osbornes) and went in dower with his daughter Margaret to Richard Fitz Pontz or des Ponts.

Walter, the second son of this marriage, was called at first Fitz Richard Fitz Ponts, but afterwards, on succeeding to the property of his mother, assumed the surname de Clifford from the place of his residence. His eldest daughter was the ill-fated favourite of Henry II. Her birthplace is involved in as much obscurity as the rest of her history. Not Clifford only, but Frampton-on-Severn, Hay Castle and Hamnash Clifford near Leominster contend for the honour of having produced " the

Fair Rosamond." The evidence seems most in favour of the first-named place, which was the ordinary seat of the family. The story of the labyrinth at Woodstock and the poisoned draught to which her death is ascribed belong rather to the region of romance than to that of history. With regard to the latter point the most credible chroniclers are silent and the tradition is perhaps due to the fact that at Godstowe Nunnery, where she was buried beside her mother, a gravestone was found on which a cup, suitable for such a purpose, was engraved.

In the Royal Collection at Hampton Court there is a so-called portrait of Fair Rosamond, which seems to resemble that which Gale, the antiquary, acquired in 1714 and of which he gives the following description :

" It is painted on a panel of wainscot and represents her in a three-quarter proportion, dressed in the habit of the times, a straight body'd gown of changeable red velvet with large square sleeves of black flowered damask facings, turned up above the bend of her arms, and close sleeves of a pearl-coloured satin puffed out but buttoned at the wrist appearing from under the large ones ; she has several rings set with precious stones on her fingers. Her breast covered with a fine flowered linen, gathered close at the neck like a ruff. Her face is charmingly fair, with a fine blush in her cheeks. Her hair of a dark brown, parted with a seam from the middle of her forehead upwards under her coifure, which is very plain, but a gold lace appears above it, and is covered with a small cap of black silk. She is looking very intensely upon the fatal cup which she holds in one hand and the cover in the other, as going to drink it. Before her is a table covered with black damask, on which there lies a prayer-book open, writt in the ancient black character ; the whole piece is extremely well preserved. I take it to have been done about Harry the 7th's time." *(Letters from the Bodleian Library, ii. 70.)* It hardly need be added that the portrait can have little claim to authenticity, though the artist may have been guided in its execution by tradition and the limning of some ancient illuminator.

Walter de Clifford, brother of the Fair Rosamond, succeeded to the estates of his father in 1221. He had sided with King John throughout his troublous reign, but joined Sir Richard Marshal, Earl of Pembroke, in his armed protest against the capricious favouritism of Henry III. The King, with his usual arbitrariness, deprived him of his estates, which he distributed among the Poictevins, but after a few months' interval restored him to favour and granted him afresh in 1234 the Castle of Clifford which had been recently given to Henry de Trubleville. An old chronicler (*Matt. Paris*) gives good evidence of the temper of this border baron by recording the fact that he was accused of having compelled the king's messenger to eat, seal and all, the royal letter which he had brought him. This *mauvaise plaisanterie* nearly cost him his life, but he was allowed, by the king's special mercy, to condone the offence by the payment of a thousand marks. In 1250 he received the king's command to effect a marriage between his only child—a girl of twelve years old—and her cousin, William Longspee, great grandson of the Fair Rosamond. Longspee was killed in a tournament at Blythe in 1256 before his father-in-law's death, and, as Walter de Clifford had no issue by his second wife (Margaret, daughter of Llywelyn, Prince of Wales), the young widow became heir to the vast possessions of the De Cliffords. She was forcibly carried off from her manor house by John Giffard of Brimsfield who afterwards obtained the king's permission to marry her.

Giffard himself was a man of mark. We find him foremost among the barons of the marches in opposing Simon de Montfort and in assisting Prince Edward in his escape from Hereford in 1265. In 1282 he joined his forces with those of Edmund Mortimer and completely defeated (near Builth) Llywelyn, the insurgent Prince of Wales. That patriot, of whom all Cambria is justly proud, met with an ignoble end. While bravely defending the bridge over the Irvon with a handful of men against the overpowering troops of English, he was surprised in the rear by a detachment under Sir Elias Walwyn. Either in the struggle that ensued or as he was escaping from it unarmed, he was mortally stabbed in the back by Adam de Frankton, who struck off his head and carried it to King Edward. The body was dragged by the soldiers a short distance to the junction of two cross roads and there buried in a spot since known by the name of Cefn y bedd, the ridge of Llywelyn's grave *(Jones's Brecknock, i. 142)*.   Matilda Longspee, wife of the victor and kinswoman of the vanquished,   implored Archbishop Peckham to absolve the Welsh prince (whose death he had witnessed) and permit his re-interment in consecrated ground, but the prelate refused, alleging that he had heard no words of repentance issue from his lips in his last moments.

It may be worth mentioning that this John Giffard had license from the king in 1280 to hunt wolves with dogs and nets in all the forests of England *(Rymer's Fœdera, ii, 58)*, but whether the vast accumulations of wolves' (?) bones, which were discovered below Clifford Castle in the construction of the railway, were the result of his success in the chase we must leave others to determine.

Giffard died in 1299, when the heirs of his first wife Matilda de Clifford, were found to be Margery, wife of the Earl of Lincoln (to whom she had been affianced when she was five years old) and Matilda's three daughters by John Giffard.   Between these co-heirs the Barony of Brimsfield continues in abeyance, the representatives of the latter being the Lords Audley Stourton, and Petre.

Clifford was afterwards granted by the crown to the Mortimers, and the Castle gave a night's shelter to King Richard II and his uncle, John of Gaunt, in 1381.   After it had become the property of the Crown by the accession of the House of York (in which the family of Mortimer was merged) we find the Castle mentioned from time to time in the public records.   The ill-fated Henry Stafford, Duke of Buckingham, was its constable in the first year of King Edward IV's reign, and Edward Croft held the same office in the reign of Henry VII, but there is no reason to suppose that either of them ever resided in the place. Indeed Powell, who visited and sketched the ruins some sixty years ago, states that there were then growing upon the Castle site, oak trees which must be 300 or 400 years old. *(Add MS. 17,458)*.   These have now disappeared, though there are still some fine ashes and other trees in the field adjoining the Castle mound and which perhaps once formed its outermost ward.

The remains of the Castle consist chiefly of a fragment of the northern wall, very massive, and standing at the extreme edge of a steep escarpment, partly natural and partly formed by the railway cutting. At the north-west angle is a round tower with widely splayed slits in its two stories, over which and the adjoining western wall the ivy grows in great luxuriance. Powell (from whose sketch in the British Museum Library our illustration is taken) was able to trace some vestiges of the barbican, but these have now wholly disappeared together with most of the eastern square tower which perhaps was the original keep. The earliest period to which we can assign any of the existing remains is the reign of Edward I, and we can only conjecture that the fortress was a quadrangular building with two baileys, environed on its landward sides by a wet moat communicating with the river Wye.

The Castle seems to have been only occasionally tenanted in the fifteenth century and thus gradually fell into disrepair. Neglect and exposure have probably effected in this instance what has been caused elsewhere by the hand of man. The existence of some of the border castles it must be remembered was in all probability a very brief one and so soon as the union between England and Wales had been thoroughly cemented they were left to perish merely because their 'raison d'être' was gone.

Mr. J. H. Parker in his Domestic Architecture (*vol ii, p. 20*) has also some pertinent observations which are worthy of notice :—

"Although the great hall at Newcastle was erected in the reign of Henry III., the other works which had assimilated that fortress in plan to the Welsh Castles were executed in the time of Edward I, and yet we see that in about half a century the whole place was ruinous and scarcely habitable. 'This fact' (viz. that such buildings were often reared in a hasty and careless manner or else were wilfully dilapidated) 'is still more strikingly apparent in the history of some of the Edwardian

Castles in Wales, that of Conway, for example. Little more than twenty years after the completion of Conway Castle, viz. in 1343, a survey of that building was made under a royal commission,' which shewed that it already needed most extensive repairs the cost of which was estimated at £425 10s. 'It is obvious from these facts that there was some radical defect in the method of building practised by our ancestors or that their materials were bad. At the same time much damage would arise from the imperfect exclusion of the weather by unglazed windows, and as the roofs are generally described as ruinous there arises a natural suspicion that the keepers of the castles sometimes made away with the lead that originally covered them.' "

The manor of Clifford, in which were included the remains of the Castle, was granted in 1547 to Lord Clinton, in consideration of his services against the Scots in the memorable battle of Musselburgh. It remained, however, a very short time in the possession of his family, for though the gallant peer (ancestor of the Duke of Newcastle) was enriched by royal grants to an almost unparalleled extent, yet his son the second earl, by his lavish expenditure dissipated much of his inheritance and actually suffered from pecuniary embarrassment. (See Lodge's illustrations, vol. iii).

The ruins of Clifford Castle are protected from further decay by their present owner, Tomkyns Dew Esq., whose grandfather inherited them from the Wardour family. (see Whitney, infra.)

Comfort Castle

Is said to have existed during the Saxon Era in the immediate neighbourhood of Leominster. It must be remembered that in præ-Norman times a Castle generally consisted of earthworks defended by a ditch and wooden palisades, and that as stone entered very little, if at all, into its construction no ruins (in the strict sense of the word) could long survive; Leland, writing early in the sixteenth century, says "The common fame of the people about Lemster is that king Merwald *(see Kingsland)* and some of his successors had a castle or palace on a hill side by the Town of Lemster, half a mile off by east. The place is now called Comfort Castle where now be some tokens of Ditches where buildings have been. The Town people and others thereabouts come once a year to this place to sport and play." Blount further tells us that at the close of the following century "the tradition touching the Castle was almost worn out and the yearly solemnity of sports there discontinued. But the place pointed at must in all likelihood be that mount which overlooks Hay lane and, in truth, that great ridge of hills now in possession of Wallop Brabazon Esq. were anciently called the Castle of Comfort hills and were heretofore given for maintenance of a chantry priest in Ludlow Church, and as such were granted by Edward VI to John Cupper and Richard Trevor, gent, aº 7 Ed. VI." *(Blount's MS)*.

As there are absolutely no remains in existence nor any other data than the above upon which to base a theory, we will only suggest that the spot may have been occupied by Offa in the lengthened warfare which he waged against the native tribes.

Croft Castle

DERIVES its chief interest from the history of the family which, according to the received tradition, retained possession of it for more than seven centuries.

In the Domesday Survey it is stated that one Bernard held Croft under William de Scotries and that, in the time of Edward the Confessor, it belonged to Earl Edwin. The Croft family claim this Bernard as their ancestor, and even adduce a more remote progenitor who, with some contempt for the history of titles, is styled 'Sir Jasper a Croft.' * As, however, such assertions do not admit of proof we must be content to observe that the *name* is undoubtedly Saxon, and that we know on the best authority (*Bracton, Coke, Littleton, 116, b.*) that there were instances at the Norman Conquest of Saxon Thanes who, after having been ousted of their lordship by Norman intruders, held by villenage the same lands which they had previously enjoyed as freemen. In all such instances, however, the entry in Domesday is very different from that which we have quoted and we must therefore conclude that Bernard occupied Croft under other circumstances than these, though he might subsequently, either by marriage or purchase, have regained possession of lands of which his ancestors had been temporarily deprived. But, as has been already observed. these are

---

* *Vincent, Visit. of Salop* mentions in the Harley pedigree Sir Jasper Croft who, attending Godfrey de Bouillon in the Crusades (1098), was made a knight of the Holy Sepulchre.

Croft. 1850

at the best theories incapable of absolute proof, and we can do no more than mention them, together with the current tradition that it was a Croft whom the Marchers selected in 1265 for the hazardous enterprise of delivering Prince Edward from his imprisonment at Hereford, in commemoration of which event a lion was added to the arms of the Croft family. *(See under Wigmore.)*

To come to ascertained facts we learn from the Public Records *(Lib. Scacc.)* that, as early as the reign of Henry III, Hugo of that ilk held Croft by military service of the honour of Dilewe or Dilwyn. The amount of land thus occupied was one hide,—equivalent to about 120 acres. We meet with another Hugo de Croft in the Rolls of Parliament as the representative of Herefordshire in the eight year of Edward II (1314-1315,) and either he, or one of the same name, is recorded as holding of King Edward III half a knight's fee in Warton and Newton, *de veteri feoffamento. i.e.*, by descent from the time of Henry I. *(Liber. Scutag., 1 Edw. iii.)*

The antiquity of the family is therefore well established by unimpeachable evidence, and it may be safely asserted that from the twelfth till the close of the eighteenth century the Crofts have been landholders in the county, often occupying the leading offices there, and, as the following notes will show, acquiring for themselves no little distinction in the annals of the nation.

Sir John de Croft, 'sometime Governor of Merk Castle in France, and frequently employed in negotiations in Flanders, between 1402 and 1404,' is stated in the family pedigree to have married Janet, one of the daughters and co-heirs of the renowned Owen Glendower, the other co-heirs being the wives of Scudamore and Monnington respectively. We may perhaps trace something of the bold chieftain's spirit in their descendants,—indeed, in two of the grandchildren of Sir John it may be said to have displayed itself in equally marked but widely differing ways.

Richard Croft, the elder grandchild, captured Prince Edward, son of Henry VI, at the battle of Tewkesbury, and for the valour that he displayed

against the insurgents under Lambert Simnel was made a Knight Banneret
upon the field of Stoke by Henry VII.   His younger brother, Thomas
Croft, who had been appointed by Edward IV and again by Richard III
ranger of Woodstock park *(Pat. Rolls 4 Edw. IV, 1 Ric. III)*, was
in 1491 deprived of this and every other place of trust and honour because
he had "commytted a detestable murdre within the Marches of Wales and
therefore fledde and tooke the sayntuary of Beaudely." *(Rot. Parl. VI
403.)* Such deeds of violence were by no means rare in the days when civil
war had kindled the passions and divided the interests of nearest neighbours.
Mr. Wright in his history of Ludlow cites an Act of Parliament in
which the whole family of Kinaston, one of the highest standing in
Shropshire, was held up to public odium on account of the 'murthers and
robberies and other great and inordynat offences commytted by them.'

In the sixteenth century the family of Croft produced its most
distinguished member, around whose career a considerable amount both
of interest and contradiction hangs.

James Croft was the only son of Richard Croft of Croft Castle by
Catharine daughter of Richard Herbert, of Montgomery.   He entered on
public life in 1542 being then returned, in conjunction with John Vaughan,
as M.P. for Herefordshire, and nine years afterwards was appointed by
King Edward VI Lord deputy of Ireland.   He retained that office only
one year and in 1552 was made Deputy-Constable of the Tower of
London—a mark of great trust inasmuch as it appears that he was still a
supporter of the un-reformed Church.   It has been assumed that he held this
important post in the interest of Lady Jane Grey *(Townsend's Leominster,
p. 67.)*, but contemporary authorities contradict the assumption.   Strype
distinctly states that he was removed by Edward VI in June 1553
(Memorials, p. 425.) and there can be little doubt that in the following
January he was foremost in the demonstration in favour of Queen Jane
which was made in Herefordshire.   This was speedily crushed, but we
find him on the 21st Feb. 1554 brought to the Tower as a prisoner by
the Sheriff of Salop.   He was examined on the charge of having taken
part in Wyatt's rebellion and condemned, but was permitted to escape

with his life and was released from imprisonment on the 1st of January 1555. *(see Chronicle of Queen Jane; Camden Soc. Vol. XLVIII)*. His after-life was equally chequered. Queen Elizabeth had him in favour and appointed him Governor of Berwick. "At the siege of Leith, he behaved himself most valiantly in repelling the foe, and yet, when in a second assault the English were worsted, the blame fell upon him (as if he favoured the French and maligned the Lord Gray, their general), so that he was outed of his government of Berwick. Yet he fell not so into the Queen's final disfavour, but that she continued him privy counsellor and made him comptroller of her household. He was an able man to manage war, and yet an earnest desirer and advancer of peace, being one of the commissioners in 1588 to treat with the Spaniards in Flanders." *(Fuller's Worthies.)* To this, however, it must be added that Mr. Froude, the historian, has recently discovered among the records at Simancas some papers which tend to qualify this favourable verdict. From them it appears that Sir James concealed his adherence to the old religion and was in Philip's pay, betraying his mistress's secrets and using his influence to mislead her. Sir James Croft was buried in Westminster Abbey 1597 under a plain gravestone, with an inscription merely stating the office he held at his death.

His grandson and successor Sir Herbert Croft, a courtier and member of Parliament, "being full weary of the vanities and fooleries of this world did retire to Douay in Flanders and there was in 1617 received among the brethren in the College of English Benedictines ; who appointing him a little cell within the ambits of their house, he spent the remainder of his days therein in strict devotion and religious exercise." *(Wood's Ath. Oxon.)*

Sir Herbert's three sons were all men of mark. The eldest, Sir William Croft, sacrificed his life and fortune for the Royal cause. He was a prisoner at the siege of Hereford in 1643 and two years afterwards was slain, fighting for his King, at Stoke Say Castle in Shropshire. *

---

* It is remarkable that Sir William's epitaph in Croft Church is incorrect in two particulars. It states that he was killed in 1641 "leading the Luston men into a field near Hopton Castle." All contemporary authorities agree in the version given in the text.

Clement Barkesdale, the rhyming Rector of Sudely, commemorates him in some lines more remarkable for their quaintness than for their poetry :—

> " Quoth I have forgot the Castle now
> Where Skydmore's men met such an overthrow,
> The wisest are not (as we see of late)
> Or valiantest, ever the most fortunate.
> But perish may the place, perish the day
> When sober Croft came to such a fray.
> Name me not Birch, nor Morgan, there
> Where Croft was slain they conquered Herefordshire.
> There was more wit and valour in that one
> And one more prisoner, than in all that run.
> Thou wer't preserved a prisoner to tell
> How sadly Croft, how honorably fell :
> Let not the pair of virtuous sisters hear
> Till the good Dean his Cordials prepare."

" The good Dean " was Sir William's brother, Herbert Croft, successively Dean and Bishop of Hereford. Although brought up at Douay he became an attached member of the Church of England and was chosen by Charles I to be one of his chaplains. For piety, zeal, and devotion to the best interests of his diocese Bishop Croft yields to none who have ever filled the episcopal throne. That his courage was equal to that of his soldier brothers is proved by his sermon against sacrilege preached in the presence of Colonel Birch and his fanatic followers, and by the boldness which he shewed in rebuking the king in his sermons before him. He set a good example by conferring the dignities of the cathedral only upon residents within his diocese "that the duty of the church might not be neglected, and the small livings augmented," and his own time was almost wholly spent amongst those whose oversight had been committed to him. Like his contemporary the equally loyal man of Ross, he was fond of planting, and the chesnut avenues which are among the beauties of Croft and Aymestry still survive to testify to his taste.

The sacrifices made by the Croft family for their king were inadequately recompensed by the grant of a Baronetcy to the good Bishop's son and heir, who sat in Parliament for many years both before and after the Revolution as member for Herefordshire—a distinction to which his descendant, the present Baronet, has been recently elected.

Sir Archer Croft, the third Baronet, was compelled by straitened means to part with his ancestral property in 1746. Mr. Yate, the mortgagee, surrendered his purchase to Mr. Richard Knight, the celebrated iron master of Downton, who had large claims upon the Croft estate. The only daughter of Mr. Knight's eldest son eventually inherited it and marrying Thomas Johnes Esq. of Hafod carried Croft into that family. Within the Castle were born Col. Johnes the accomplished translator of Froissart and his brother Mr. Johnes Knight who is said to have married George IV. to Mrs. Fitzherbert. Col. Johnes sold Croft to Mr. Somerset Davies of Wigmore, the maternal grandfather of its present proprietor, the Rev. William Kevill Davies.

Mr. Wright (*Hist. of Ludlow, p 85,*) considers it likely that a Castle was erected at Croft in Norman or even in præ-Norman times, but there are certainly no traces now extant of any building earlier than the fourteenth century. Judging from the angle towers and other indications of the form of the fortress we should assign it to the later Edwardian era, but the destruction which overtook it in the Civil wars was so complete and the notices of it in Records are so scanty that it is impossible to speak with any confidence.

It is a quadrangular building with circular towers at the four corners, enclosing a courtyard. In the middle of the last century there was no wall between the two eastern towers, and access to the house was then gained through the open courtyard—the door being upon the *inner* side of the western wing. Possibly this may indicate that the transformation of the Castle into a dwelling house was effected by Sir James Croft in the time of Queen Elizabeth, when, in compliment to the sovereign, it was customary to construct buildings in the form of the letter E.   Leland, in his tour through England early in the sixteenth century, observed on his way from Eaton to Ludlow "Croft, the manor of the Crofts, set on the brow of the hill, ditched and walled castle-like," but he did not visit it nor does he give any further details about it.   In the year 1645 the Royal troops (Symonds says, "the Ludlow men") thought it prudent to dismantle the Castle lest the enemy should seize on it for their own uses, *(Symonds's Diary, p. 203.)* and no doubt it underwent many changes when it was subsequently refitted.   The portion that seems to have suffered least is the northern side (now occupied as offices), where there is a square centre turret midway between the two angle towers.   Mr. Knight made considerable alterations immediately after it came into his hands and by Mr. Johnes the eastern side was rebuilt and the whole fabric greatly modernised.   The West Hall is probably the original Hall of the Castle but curtailed in its dimensions at its southern extremity, and the angle towers are now all that remains to testify to the earlier character of the building.

Cublington Castle

OR Cubbeston, in the Parish of Madley, still retains the name of a Castle, although all traces of the fortified building have long since disappeared.

A division of the Royal Army was quartered at Madley in the autumn of 1645 and that industrious antiquary Richard Symonds, (who commanded a troop of horse), carefully examined the Church and would doubtless have mentioned the existence of any ruins within the parish had such been visible. Probably the Castle was then in much the same state as thirty years afterwards, when Blount speaks of it as a moated manor house in the occupation of Bodenham Gunter, gent. *(Blount's MS.)*

Symonds's notes, however, enable us to suggest that its occupants in feudal times were the Delafields—a knightly family which "built part of the faire Church" of Madley and was commemorated in one of its windows. A few fragments only now remain of the painted glass which in his day depicted the kneeling figure of a knight in complete armour, with hands upraised in the attitude of prayer, his sword suspended from a highly enriched belt and his surcoat embroidered with sable three garbs argent. Beneath were the words **Walt'us et Joh'es Felde.** *(Symonds's Diary, Camd. Soc. vol. LXXIV., p. 232.)* We find John de le Feld, Richard de le Feld, clerk, and John ap Rees associated with Kynard Delabere (the owner of Tibberton) in the foundation of a chantry to the B. V. Mary in Madley Church in 1394, *(Harl. MS. 6726)*, and these were no doubt members of the same family which intermarried with the Fitzwarines and subsequently with the Butlers of Kilpeck Castle.

Cublington is now a Prebend of Hereford Cathedral, having been formed out of Preston Prebend at a comparatively recent date.

Cusop Castle.

◆•◆

THE etymology of Cusop accurately describes its position in the hollow at the junction of two hills, or ranges of hills; the situation of the Castle, a little to the south west of the Church, is therefore wanting in the dignity which the entrenchment (called Mouse Castle) on the summit of a neighbouring hill possesses. Cusop Castle was probably nothing more than a Pele tower or tower-built house, strong enough to resist the attack of any band of marauders, but unfitted to endure a regular siege. The area encircled by the moat and earthworks is estimated to have been an acre in extent and was no doubt occupied by stabling and outbuildings which, until the fifteenth century, were usually of wood. (see Parker's Domestic Architecture, ii. 12). Some rough stonework, the only remains of the Castle Walls, was visible within the memory of man (or rather of one old woman), but the demands of parish roads and farm-house repairs have assisted Nature in the task of demolition.

Silas Taylor briefly describes both the Camp (which is perhaps the strongest in the county) and the Castle in these terms :— "The two Castles, that of Llwygod which is on the extremity of an hill, doubly intrenched ; and the Castle by the Church, and with large banks moated, seemes to be securityes made for defence in the Welsh turmoyles ; the first carrying the name of an *Eye* by reason of the height which administered convenience of viewing." (*Harl. MS. 6726.*)

The earliest occupants of the Castle of whom we have any record were the de Clanowes, or de Clavenoghs, whose names occur among the representatives of the county during the reigns of Edward II and III and Richard II.

One of this family, Philip de Clavenogh, was an adherent of the Earl of Lancaster in the Barons' wars, and took part in the rather summary act of justice by which Piers Gaveston, the favourite of Edward II, lost his life on the scaffold. The king pardoned him, but could not detach him from the Baronial party, and we find him following the Earl of Hereford, who had joined Lancaster in his opposition to the Despensers, and again committing felonies for which he needed and obtained the royal pardon. *(Parl. Writs.)* Edward's clemency was so readily bestowed that one cannot but suspect the motive which prompted it. Philip's son, Sir John Clanowe, Knight of the Chamber, was associated in the reign of Richard II with another Herefordshire Knight, Sir Nicholas Sarnesfield, K.G., in a somewhat curious mission. They were to notify to Sir William le Scrope (afterwards Earl of Wiltshire) the award of the King in Council, that the jewel which Scrope was to offer at the Shrine of St. Cuthbert at Durham, as a penance for certain transgressions and misprisions committed against Walter the Bishop of that see, should not be of less value than £500. *(Beltz, Order of the Garter. p. 309.)* An heiress of the Clanowe family married Sir John Pointz of Iron Acton, but the next possessor of Cusop about whom we have been able to obtain any information is Henry ap Griffith, Lord of the manor temp. Edw. IV, 'whom tradition sayeth was owner of Newcourt in the valley of Doure.' *(Harl. MS. 6726.)* He was the ancestor of a branch of the Vaughan family through whom the property, united with Dorston, Moccas and Bredwardine, descended to an heiress who married Cornewall. Sir George Cornewall, Bart., at the beginning of the present century parted with it, in exchange, to Mr. Walter Watkins. *(Duncumb ii. 286.)*

Dorston Castle.

◆•◉•◆

THE obvious derivation of this name from the Celtic *dwr* (water) and the Saxon *ton* (enclosure) is favoured by the situation of the place on the river Dore at the head of the Golden Valley. It has, however, been suggested with some plausibility that both Dorston and the neighbouring cromlech called Arthur's stone are but corruptions of Thorstein, the stone or altar of Thor, and perhaps to favour this theory Duncumb rashly identifies Dorstone with the Torches-stone of Domesday, The latter place is however in Stratford Hundred which by no possibility could be extended so as to include Dorston, and we may readily account for the absence of that name from the Survey by the fact that the Chatellany of Clifford comprehended within its limits several manors not specifically described.

The Castle of Dorston is not mentioned in the earliest Rolls, but in the thirteenth and fourteenth centuries seems to have formed the residence of the family of Solers (de Solariis), a family to whose importance the names of Bridge-Solers and Sollars-Dilwyn in this county and Neen-Solers in Shropshire abundantly testify, and which survived at Pentre-Solers in Glasbury till the 17th century. Silas Taylor *(Harl. MS. 6726)* extracts from the Register of Bishop Trillec the following curious story. "In 1346 William Solers, lord of Dorston, and John Eggesworth chaplain to the Cantary which the ancestors of the said Will. Solers founded, fell out about some of the profitts belonging to the foundation and it grew so high that by force William seized the lands and kept the profitts soe that there was high doings, which comeing to ye Bishop's eares at that time, he gives an order and in it enjoynes the Deacon (Dean) of Webbely to seize on the profitts and sequester them to his use and soe they two snarling at another the Bishop went away with the Bone "!

In 1399 we find Johannes de Solers returned as holding Dorston under Mortimer of Wigmore, but in 1403 Henry IV entrusted the Castle to Sir Walter Fitzwalter *(Rymer's Fœdera, viii, 328)*, desiring him to strengthen it, as the neglected condition of the Border Castles had encouraged Glendwr to make his successful attack on the English counties. Fitzwalter was a Baron of no mean reputation as a warrior, but the English troops distributed throughout the Marches were too few to keep in check the Welsh insurgents. In the following year Glendwr made himself master of the whole of Wales and "all the summer plundered, burnt and destroyed the districts around him . . . . and took many castles, some of which he levelled with the ground, while he fortified others for himself. *(Walsingham, p. 562.)*

Dorston probably met with the former fate, as we find no further allusion to it as a fortress, though even as late as the seventeenth century it retained the name of a Castle and may possibly have afforded a night's shelter to King Charles I. Symonds tells us that on "Wednesday, Sept. 17 (1645). The whole army mett at a rendesvouz upon Arthurstone Heath neare Durston Castle, com. Hereford ; and from thence his majestie marched to Hom Lacy, the seat of the Lord Viscount Scudamore." *(Diary p. 240.)*

The lordship of Dorston Castle changed hands very frequently. Lady Fitzwalter died seised of it about the year 1422 *(Inq. p.m. 1 Hen. vi)* but soon afterwards it belonged to Richard de la Mare, an Agincourt hero, whose death in 1435 is commemorated by a beautiful brass in the Cathedral. *(Inq. p.m. 14 Hen. vi.)* Its subsequent possessors were the Lysters who sold it in the reign of Elizabeth to Morgan Aubrey—father of Sir Samuel Aubrey to whom a tablet in the Cathedral attributes every virtue,—from whose descendant, Richard Aubrey of Clehonger, it was purchased in 1780 by the Cornewall family, and now belongs to Sir George Cornewall, Bart.

Eardisley Castle.

◆·●·◆

IN the Domesday Survey 'Herdeslege' is described under the possessions of Roger de Laci as situated in the middle of a forest of which we may see the last survivor in the celebrated oak which is still flourishing. The Castle is called 'a defensible mansion' and at that early period probably partook more of the character of a Saxon earth and timber work than of a Norman fortalice. Its occupant was one Robert and in Edward the Confessor's time Earl Edwin held it. It seems probable that it was converted into a regular fortress as early as the twelfth century, and at the commencement of the reign of Henry III it is returned in a list of Herefordshire Castles. Situated in the rich valley of the Wye and on the high road into England, Eardisley was exposed to frequent attacks from Welsh marauders and was also in the very centre of the districts where the Barons' wars were waged with the utmost violence. How many times it changed hands in that troublous time it would be very difficult to ascertain, for the King had so slight a hold on the nobility that the same Barons appear alternately as his partizans and his enemies, and the Castle which to-day opposed the insurgents might to-morrow afford them a friendly shelter.

In the year 1262 the Welsh were in open insurrection and under the leadership of Llywelyn made their way towards Hereford, plundering Eardisley and Weobley in their course and driving Roger de Mortimer, the king's chief supporter, into his Castle at Wigmore.

At the close of that year the Cathedral city was itself threatened and Bishop Aquablanca, unpopular alike from being one of the king's foreign favourites and a most inefficient prelate, applied to Henry III for support. Measures were immediately taken to check the progress of the Welsh, but Llywelyn had meanwhile made common cause with Simon de Montfort and the insurgent Barons and, defeating Mortimer, ravaged the lands of the king's partizans. Macy de Bezile, the foreign sheriff of Gloucester, was seized and with the obnoxious Bishop of Hereford, who had been haled from the very altar of his Cathedral, was imprisoned in the Castle of Eardisley. In whose hands the Castle at this time happened to be is, for the reasons already given, somewhat hard to ascertain. Probably it belonged to the de Bohuns, for it would appear that they were its chief lords throughout the thirteenth century and that Humphry de Bohun, the eldest son of the Earl of Hereford, obtained by his marriage with Eleanor de Braose most of the county which lies between the Arrow and the Wye. *(see Huntington.)* The de Bohuns were on the whole the most consistent supporters of the Baronial cause in Herefordshire and the Welsh Marches, fighting at Evesham and Lewes in the foremost ranks of the insurgent army, generally with success but occasionally suffering a temporary check. Thus in 1277, when the sceptre had fallen from the imbecile hands of Henry III into the vigorous grasp of Edward I, Eardisley Castle was taken from them and given to Roger de Clifford who had shewn himself a staunch adherent of the royal cause. A few years later the de Bohuns regained their position and continued lords of Eardisley till the extinction of the Earldom of Hereford in 1372, when the lordship of Eardisley vested in the crown. *(Extenta 39 Edw. iii.)* We find that in 1375 on the death of Richard de Baskerville, Chivalier, the mesne lord of Eardisley, the jurors declared (though the fact was disputed by Sir John de Poyntz) that it was held by him of the heirs of Humphry de Bohun, late Earl of Hereford, and of William de Ferrers deceased, who were the tenants *in capite* of the crown (*Placita, p. 390*). From this we gather that Eardisley had belonged originally to Richard Marshal, Earl of Pembroke, from two of whose daughters and co-heirs Bohun and Ferrers each derived his interest.

We must now give some account of the mesne lords of Eardisley, the Baskervilles, (a Norman family either from Basqueville in the Pays de Caux or Boscherville near Rouen) whose connection with the place commenced at least as early as the thirteenth century. In 1251 Humphry de Bohun and Aleanore his wife, by a fine granted the manor of 'Irdesle' to Walter de Baskerville *(Close Rolls 36 Hen. iii. m. 16)* but there is good reason to believe that his ancestors had been settled in that place— certainly in the county—at a much earlier date. They claim, indeed, to have acquired possession of the manor of Eardisley by the marriage of Sir Ralph Baskerville with Sibyl, heiress of Adam de Port and of his wife who was a daughter of de Braose and a grand-daughter of Milo, Earl of Hereford; nor must we omit Camden's statement that "they deduce their pedigree from a niece of Dame Gunora, that most famous lady in Normandy." *(Camden's Britannia.)* With greater certainty we may state that Ralph de Baskerville held lands under Adam de Port *de veteri feoffamento, i.e.* by inheritance from the reign of Henry I *(Lib. Scut.)* and that on the murder of Ralph Baskerville in Northamptonshire about the year 1194 his son Thomas succeeded him at Pickthorn, the Shropshire estate *(Eyton's Shropshire),* and another son, Roger, at Eardisley in Herefordshire. *(Her. Visit.)*

Walter de Baskerville, grandson of this Roger, had licence from the Bishop of Hereford in 1272 "to hold divine service in an oratory built within the walls of the Castle" *(Reg. Breton*), and we may assume from this that Eardisley had then become the chief residence of the family, as it continued to be for the four succeeding centuries.

During that long period the house of Baskerville produced a series of knights, whom to mention by name would exceed our limits. They won their spurs not by wealth or by waiting upon the Court, but by active service at home and abroad, and on the grave of each might be inscribed the quaint old epitaph :—

> *Eques Auratus* well may he be said
> Whose coyne, not warlike courage, such hath made ;
> To Baskerville, we *Miles* do afford
> As knighted on the field by his flesht sword.

The most eminent members of the Eardisley line were Sir John Baskerville who, while yet a boy, followed King Henry to the battle field of Agincourt and his son, Sir James, one of the three Herefordshire heroes who were made Knights Banneret by Henry VII after the battle of Stoke in 1487. The latter married Sibyl, sister of Walter Devereux, first Lord Ferrars, who fell at Bosworth fighting against the cause which his brother-in-law supported. A descendant was Sir Thomas Baskerville who died in 1597 commanding Queen Elizabeth's troops in Picardy. There was a tablet to his memory in old St. Paul's setting forth the glories of 'the right worthy and valient Gentleman' and his services in the Netherlands, Indies, Spain, and France and attributing to him

'A pure regarde to the immortall parte
A spotless minde and an unvanquisht hart.'

In the Civil war Sir Humphrey Baskerville of Eardisley took the side of the king but was not actively engaged in the struggle. Indeed, the importance of the family had then begun to decline and Symonds states that the income of the knight (whom he calls a traveller) had dwindled down from £3000 per annum to £300. *(Symonds's Diary p. 196.)* Misfortunes continued to attend the family. The Castle was burnt to the ground in the Civil war, only one of the gatehouses escaping, and in this the representative of the family was living in 1670 in comparative poverty. *(Blount's MS.)* The Parish Register contains the burial entry of Benhail Baskerville in 1684 to whose name are added the words 'Dominus Manerii de Erdisley.' At his death the family became extinct in the direct male line, and the remainder of the property (most of which had been sold by Sir Humphrey Baskerville in the reign of James I) was purchased by William Barnesley, Bencher of the Inner Temple. His son, having offended his father by a marriage with a portionless London girl, was disinherited either in fact or in intention and the estate became the subject of tedious litigation, the details of which may be found by those interested in *causes celebres* in the *Gentleman's Magazine, Vol. 61.* William Barnesley, junior, was weak in mind and body but his wife fought the battle manfully and celebrated the legal triumph by inscribing on their grave stone,

—'at length they overcame and died conquerors.'
' " Blessed are they which die in the Lord." '

The heir of Barnesley was a lunatic and the Castle and Park were sold to Dr. Pettit, from whom they were purchased by Mr. Perry who bequeathed them to W. Perry Herrick, Esq. of Beaumanoir, Leicestershire, their present possessor.

The Castle stood upon the western side of the Church on high ground insulated by a triple moat. The mound on which the donjon stood and the wet ditches which encircle it are all the traces of the ancient fortress which now exist. Not a fragment of the Castle remains and even the few chiselled stones which are visible in the Farm house walls seem rather to have belonged to the Manor House which occupied the Castle site than to the older building. Spear heads and armour have been found from time to time in the inner moat and the labourers employed in cleansing it a few years ago, discovered a massive piece of masonry which had probably formed a part of the ancient draw-bridge or sluice-gate.

Eaton Tregoz

IS a manor in the parish of Foy, and derives its second name from a family which held a distinguished place in the annals of the thirteenth century. The origin of the family is not very clear, but its connection with Herefordshire may with much probability be referred to the reign of King John when Robert de Tregoz, (Sheriff of Wilts 3 Ric. I) was married to Sibyl, daughter and heiress of Robert de Ewyas. *(see Ewyas Harold.)* Their son, Robert de Tregoz, was one of the most powerful barons on the Welsh Marches and gave his support to Simon de Montfort in his long struggle with Henry III. He carried the standard at Evesham and fell at that celebrated battle which was fatal to the baronial cause. His elder son, John de Tregoz, did homage to the king and was received into such favour by him that a portion of the fine incurred by his father's treason was remitted. He married Mabel daughter of the illustrious Fulk Fitzwarine, who was his near neighbour. *(see Tretire.)* Tregoz most probably resided at Eaton, where in the year 1280 he was permitted to endow a chapel within his castle and dedicate it to St. John the Baptist. *(Reg Cantilupe.)*

In the great struggle for independence which was made by the Welsh in 1282, Tregoz must have had a difficult part to play. Bound by ties of kindred to Llywelyn and by those of allegiance and gratitude to Edward he must have responded to the king's summons to join him on the border with but half a heart, and we can well believe that he fought with far better spirit, though with less success, in the unfortunate

French campaign of 1294. That his services there were not unimportant we may gather from the fact that the king permitted his wife and family to reside in the castle of Devizes, and to have fuel for their fires there, during the absence of the Baron on foreign service. His sword was once more employed in the Scottish wars and could have been hardly sheathed when death overtook him. He died in 1299 or 1300 seized of the castle of Ewyas Harold and of the manor of Eton Tregoz, and was succeeded in the latter estate by William de Grandison (see *Asperton*) who had married the younger of his two daughters and coheirs.

In the year 1309 de Grandison obtained a license from King Edward II to crenellate his mansion at Eton, and that property probably continued with his descendants until the extinction of the family in 1375. We then find it in the possession of Sir Hugh Waterton, a knight high in the service of John of Gaunt and extremely active in his opposition to Owen Glendwr. Sir Hugh was chamberlain to Henry Plantaganet (afterwards Henry IV) and accompanied him in 1392, in his journey to the Holy Sepulchre, and we may reasonably suppose that he took no light part in the deposition of King Richard and the establishment of Henry and the House of Lancaster on the throne of England.

Glendwr in 1402 was at the height of his power. Mortimer had utterly failed to check his advance into Herefordshire, and had himself been taken prisoner by the insurgent army. The Welsh had seized on Leominster and plundered all the surrounding country, levying heavy contributions from the Priory and the churches in the neighbourhood, and were only induced to retire into Carmarthenshire by the hope of completely ejecting the English from their strongholds in that county. In this they were successful. John Scudamore (a name familiar to Herefordshire ears) writes in July to the receiver of Brecknock to tell him that he can spare no man from Carregcennen Castle which he was holding for the King, as Owen had secured all Carmarthenshire, and was at that moment endeavouring to gain Carmarthen itself. "Wherefore" he adds "wryteth to Sir Hugh Waterton, and to alle thilke that ye suppose wol take this matter to hart, that thei excite the kyng hederwardes in al haste to vengen hym on summe of his false traytors the which he hath overmoche cherischid, and to rescewe the townes and castels in these countrees : for I drede ful sore that there be too few trewe men in hem." *(Ellis's Original Letters, 2nd series, i. 13.)*

Whether through Waterton's urgent representations or for other reasons, Henry immediately gathered an army at Chester to chastise the Welsh chieftain, but the campaign was barren of results and at its close Glendower had made an alliance with Edmund Mortimer and the Percies which greatly increased his strength. In 1404 Sir Hugh Waterton was made a Privy Councillor and five years afterwards died, seised of the manors of Credenhill and Eton Tregoz and the advowson of the chapel of Eton, county Hereford. By his wife Ellen daughter of Robert Mowbray he left two co-heirs, Blanche, the wife of Sir Robert Challons and Elizabeth, who married John ap Harry, of Poston, in the Golden Valley.

A little later in the fifteenth century John Abrahall became possessed of Eton Tregoz. He served as knight of the shire in 1431 and died seised of Eton in 1443, William Abrahall being his son and heir. *(Pedes Finium 22 Hen. VI.)* The Abrahalls continued at Eton for three centuries, intermarrying with the Walwyns, Rudhalls, Kyrles, Hoskynses, and other ancient Herefordshire families, but not producing any single member of much eminence. The last male heir of Eton branch, the Rev. George Abrahall, died in 1673 and his co-heirs divided the property. The elder married Colonel Bubb (father by his second wife of that busy politician Bubb Dodington, Lord Melcombe) and the younger married the Rev. William Jones, whose grandson was the eventual heir of the family.

Eccleswall Castle.

◆·•·◆

WHETHER England or Normandy was the cradle of the illustrious race of Talbot is a question yet undecided, but Herefordshire may at any rate claim to have been its nursery and to have sent forth a series of warriors whose martial fame culminated in the first and greatest Earl of Shrewsbury.

Richard de Talbot, the earliest known ancestor of the family in Herefordshire, obtained from King Henry II a grant of the lordship of Eccleswall and Linton, lands which perhaps his great uncle Geoffrey might have viewed with envy when he went westward to hold the Castles of Weobley and Hereford for the Empress Matilda. At Eccleswall the family seem to have settled and to have been entrusted with various important posts by which their loyalty was tested. In Llywelyn's insurrection we find Gilbert Talbot (the Second) among the king's staunchest adherents and holding in his interests the Castles of Grosmont, Skenfrith, and Monmouth. He died in 1274 leaving, by his wife Guendoline, daughter of Rhese ap Griffith, Prince of South Wales, a son Richard Talbot, who signs himself " Dominus de Eccleswall " in the famous letter to the Pope in which the Barons asserted the right of King Edward to the superior power in Scotland.

His eldest son, Sir Gilbert, joined with most of the Herefordshire Barons in supporting Thomas, Earl of Lancaster both in the execution of Piers Gaveston and in the impeachment of the Despensers. A heavy fine was inflicted upon him, but its execution was happily delayed till Edward III had ascended the throne and reversed the act of his predecessor. His career then became one of unmixed success. He was constituted Lord Chamberlain to the King and Justice of South Wales, and, besides obtaining from the Crown fresh grants of land, he procured the privilege of free warren in the manors of Eccleswall and Credenhill in Herefordshire.

On the death of Sir Gilbert in 1353 his son Sir Richard succeeded to the Talbot estates, but in consequence of his marriage with the heiress of Adamar de Valence he removed the seat of the family to the more important Castle of Goodrich, which he had with his wife. *(see Goodrich.)* Eccleswall, though it ceased to be the chief residence of his descendants, continued in their possession till the year 1616, when by the death of Gilbert Talbot, seventh Earl of Shrewsbury, without male issue, it devolved on his second daughter and co-heir Lady Elizabeth, wife of Henry Grey, eighth Earl of Kent.

In 1738 the estates of the last Duke of Kent, collaterally descended from the above, were sold and Eccleswall became the property of Mr. George Bonnar. It soon afterwards was purchased by Lord Ashburton to whose representatives it still belongs.

The site of the Castle is now occupied by a substantial farm-house and the traces of the original building which have survived are too slight to form a basis upon which to erect a surmise of its size and extent. A grass-grown moat and artificial mound are still visible, and some portion of the walls must have been standing in the last century when a silver seal of Philip de Henbury is recorded to have been found among them.

Ellingham Castle.

———◆•◆———

THE extensive parish of Much Marcle could boast in former times of possessing two Baronial residences, viz., Ellingham and Mortimer's Castle. The name of the former bears so striking a resemblance to Hellens or Hellings, (a manor within the parish), that we hazard the conjecture that its etymology is simply Helling's ham. The family of Helling, or as it is more often written Helyon, were owners of the manor of Westhide till the fifteenth century, but their connection with Marcle terminated at a much earlier date through the marriage of the heiress of Walter de Helyon with Richard Walwyn. Hellens then became the property of the Walwyns, or rather of that branch of this ancient family which had made Marcle their residence. This is the account which the Visitation Pedigrees concur in giving and which Leland adopts. Blount, however, asserts with some particularity that " Helions or Hellens, a manor which included one third of Much Marcle was possessed in Edward III's time by the Audleys." The two accounts are reconcileable by the supposition that the Helions were mesne lords under the Audleys or that the manors of Hellens and Audleys, distinct at one time, were subsequently united ; and either theory will not militate against Blount's further statement that the heirs of Audley sold Hellens to Thomas Walwyn in the fourth year of Henry IV.

There are few noble families whose early history has suffered worse at the hands of genealogists than the family of Audley. Dugdale's Baronage, a spendid work but from its very nature occasionally inaccurate, has been followed with such servility that his errors, by constant repetition, have almost acquired the sacredness of truth, and though it is beyond our province to set those errors right yet we shall endeavour to avoid them in the present case by adhering closely to proven facts.

The earliest lord of Much Marcle after the extinction of the Lacies (the grantees at the Conquest) of whom we find any record is John de Balun or de Baladun, who was a witness to Magna Charta in the ninth year of Henry III. Either he or his son was commanded by the same king in 1257 to assist Humphry de Bohun in guarding the Welsh Marches and we find his name also among the benefactors to Aconbury Priory. By his descendants numerous alienations were made and thus the great manor of Marcle became subdivided. Walter de Balun married Isolda daughter of Ralph de Mortimer and at his death about the year 1284 left his widow dower in Marcle. She took for her second husband Hugh de Audley and an enquiry was consequently made by the Escheator whether it would be for the king's damage if John de Balun, kinsman and heir of Walter, alienated to her husband in fee the land which she held in dower. *(Close Rolls.)* This alienation was effected and the result of it was the formation of the manor of Marcle Audleys. The de Baluns however, continued to hold lands in Marcle for some time after this date.

Hugh de Audley, the son of the above, was summoned to Parliament in 1317 and created Earl of Gloucester in 1337. By a charter dated Saturday in the Vigil of St. Bartholomew, 7 Edw. III, he granted to James de Audley, his nephew, and his issue the manor of Marcle, to revert, in case of failure of issue, to his own heirs. *(Lansdowne MS. 905, fol 75.)* This James de Audley was none other than Sir James Audley, K. G., the hero of Poictiers. How this gallant knight bore himself throughout that battle; how, faint and wounded, he was carried by his four squires to the cool shelter of a hedge, and, when the fight was won, what personal attentions and substantial ackowledgment of his valour he received from the Black Prince may be pleasantly read in the picturesque pages of Froissart or in the more recent annals of Edward III by Mr.

W. Longman. Sir James, in spite of his wounds, survived until 1369 doing active service to the very last and died at Fontenay-le-Compte " to the great sorrow of the Prince and Princess of Wales as well as of the barons and knights of Poitou." Neither Sir James nor his brother Sir Peter, who fought beside him at Poitiers, appear to have married, and their estates therefore passed to the issue of their uncle Hugh de Audley, viz., a daughter who married Ralph, first Earl of Stafford and one of the founders of the Order of the Garter.

Their grandson Edmund, 5th Earl of Stafford, alienated it in the fourth of Hen. IV to Thomas Walwayn (*Blount's MS.*), who seems to have been the son of Richard Walwayn who married the heiress of Helyon and a grandson of Sir Elias Walwayn, the captor of Llywelyn. The name of Walwayn or Walwyn is of frequent occurrence in the lists of Sheriffs and Knights of Herefordshire, and the family, which is said to have removed from the Flemish colony in Pembrokeshire to Hay Castle in the reign of Henry I, held extensive property in Stoke Edith, Dormington and Clifford as well as in Marcle.

In 1467 Thomas Walwayn was found by the jurors to have died seised of the whole manor of Much Marcle which he held of the King (as of the Castle of Wigmore) by fealty and an annual rent of xviii s. (*Inq. p. m.*) Hellens continued the property of the Walwyn family for several generations. Sir Richard Walwyn who died there in 1573, seised of it and of the manor of Dormington, had been knighted by Queen Mary in the first year of her reign for the services he had rendered in quelling an insurrection made in Herefordshire in the interest of Queen Jane on the death of Edward VI. The insurgents, 12,000 strong at first but rapidly diminished, intrenched themselves on an eminence about a mile west of Leominster, where they were attacked by the inhabitants of the town and a force from Hereford under the command of Walwyn, and were completely defeated and dispersed. In reward for this act of loyalty Queen Mary granted to Leominster a Charter of Incorporation in which the services of the townspeople were duly recited. Sir Richard's descendant John Walwyn of Hellens died without male issue early in the last century and the property became subdivided between his two daughters—the younger of whom married John Shepheard, Esq. whose representatives have generally borne the additional name of Walwyn and with whom the estate of Dormington remained for several generations.

The site of Ellingham Castle, says Blount, is "in a place not far from the town, now overgrown with wood and called the Quarry wood." We can hardly help suspecting that the *Quarry* which gave its name to the wood was nothing else than the Castle itself, the ruins of which must have afforded convenient material for the roadmaker and local builder.

Ewyas Harold Castle.

———➤•••◄———

ETYMOLOGISTS have disputed as much about the meaning of the word Ewyas, as antiquarians have differed with regard to the individual indicated by the name Harold. From the former controversy we may happily claim exemption, nor shall we occupy much space in discussing the latter. The Doomsday Survey states that at that time Alured de Merleberge held the Castle of Ewias from King William who had confirmed to him the grant which Earl William, the rebuilder of the Castle, had previously made. "Earl William" was William Fitzosberne, the most able and powerful of the Norman Barons. He conquered a portion of South Wales, and built Chepstow Castle to overawe the conquered territory. He was not Earl of Hereford only but Lord of the Isle of Wight and governor of Gloucester, in which county his possessions were even more extensive than in Herefordshire. *(see also Clifford.)* At the time of the survey the Earldom was in the King's hands, having been forfeited by the rebellion of Roger de Bretevil, the first Earl's son and successor, and, as we have seen, the Castle of Ewias had been granted to Alured of Marlborough. He surrendered it to Harold, who rebuilt the Castle and gave his name to it, but whose identity has been the subject of much speculation. Leland *(Itin. viii 84 b)* says "the fame is that the Castle of Mapherald" ("Map" being the British equivalent of the Norman Fitz) "was builded of Harold afore he was king, and when he overcame the Welshemen Harold gave this Castle to his bastard;" but it is obvious that such a tradition, unsupported by evidence, carries little weight with it. Our own opinion is that Harold was the son of Ralph, who had been displaced from the Earldom of Hereford to make room for the conqueror's relative, William Fitzosberne *(see Gough's Camden.)*

Harold, whoever he might have been, was probably the first resident lord of the Castle and his piety originated the religious house which rose beside the Castle walls. His son, who styles himself " Robertus de Ewyas,* filius Haraldi," founded the Abbey of Dore at the commencement of King Stephen's reign and built the parish church of Ewyas Harold. *(see paper on Ewyas Harold by Rev. W. C. Fowle in Cambr: Arch: Soc. Journal, 1868.)* In this as in many other instances the Church has survived the Castle, and the memory of its founder and his successors has been better preserved by their pious benefactions than by their many deeds of knightly prowess. *(see Aconbury Chartulary, printed in 8th Report of Public Records.)*

Sibilla de Ewyas, the eventual heiress of the family, married early in the 13th century Robert de Tregoz *(see ante pp. 57, 58),* and Ewyas Harold remained with their descendants until the property became subdivided at the death of John de Tregoz in 1300. His elder daughter and co-heir Clarice brought it in dower to her husband Roger de la Warre or le Warre, who had summons to parliament in the reigns of Edw. I and II. He was succeeded by his son John le Warre who in a deed (dated 1 Edw. II) styles himself " Seignur de Ewyas Harold" and, as such, releases the customary tenants of his manor from their ancient service, viz. "amunder le estanke del molyn le est apele Castelmelne ke esta devant la porte de la Priorie de Ewyas" *i.e.* from repairing the milldam of the Castle mill. *(Coningsby's MS.)* His grandson and successor Roger, was instrumental in making John, King of France prisoner at the battle of Poictiers, 1356, and had the crampet of that monarch's sword as a memorial of his share in the exploit, the buckle being given to his companion in arms, Sir John Pelham. The successors of both these

---

* Blount tells us that Robert de Ewyas was fined a hundred marks in the year 1176 for trespassing in the King's Forest in pursuit of game.

I

knights bore these trophies as honourable augmentations in their armorial shields. Roger le Warre died seised· of the Castle and Manor of Ewyas Harold which he held of the king in chief by the service of keeping the king's harriers ("canes Haier" *i.e.* dogs employed in the hays or game enclosures) whensoever the king came into those parts. *(Fines in Scac. pasch. 1 H. 4.)* His sons, John and Thomas, are both mentioned in the above Fine, but in the same year in which it is dated King Henry IV granted the Castle and Manor of Ewyas Harold to Sir Philip le Vache or de la Vache *(Cal. Rot. Pat.)*, who was connected with Herefordshire through his wife Elizabeth Clifford and his son-in-law Richard, Lord Grey de Wilton. Sir Philip, for his services in the French wars, his faithful custody of the royal jewels and his loyalty as governor of Calais and Guisnes was elected Knight of the Garter in 1399, but his tenure of Ewyas (probably for military purposes) was very brief, as in 1403 *(4 Hen. IV)* that Castle was intrusted to the care of Sir William Beauchamp, Lord Bergavenny, to fortify and hold against the incursions of Glendwr. *(Rymer vii. 328.)* Lord Bergavenny, who was justiciary of South Wales and governor of Pembroke and Kilgaran Castles, died in 1411 and by his own desire was buried "in the church of the Friars Preachers at Hereford, next and beneath the tomb of John de Hastings, Earl of Pembroke," his cousin and benefactor. *(Nicolas, Test. Vetusta 171 : Beltz. 231.)* His widow, Joan, daughter of Richard Fitz Alan Earl of Arundel, is stated by Leland to have purchased the. lordship of Ewyas Harold, which certainly, either on this account or in consequence of the previous grant to her husband, devolved on his kinsman and heir, Edward Nevill, 4th son of Ralph, 1st Earl of Westmoreland. He was summoned to parliament as, *jure uxoris*, Baron Bergavenny, and was present at the battle of Northampton fighting on the side of the Earl of March whom he afterwards supported on the throne with consistent allegiance. He died in 1476 seised of the Castle and Manor of Ewyas Harold, possessions which have descended without further interruption to his lineal representative the present Earl of Abergavenny.

The Castle of Ewyas Harold was unconnected with any events of historical importance. Possibly King John in one of his many visits to the Welsh border may have passed the night within the fortress and very probably Glendwr assailed it and helped to reduce its walls to the ruinous condition in which Leland found them a century later.

Charles I, with a detachment of the royal army, passed through Ewyas in the autumn of 1645, and Symonds, the antiquarian officer, noticed the Church and the Castle—the large part of which, including the chapel of St. Nicholas which Leland observed, was then "ruynous and gone." The latter term is that which, without qualification, must now be applied to it. Powell's account, written some seventy years ago, may be taken as a true picture of the present condition of the site. "From the brook or river I ascended a hill covered with bushes and trees and came on a large area of unequal ground, overgrown with fern and woods among which are some ancient oaks. Beyond, in front, appears a high mound which was the keep, also covered with woods. Not a vestige of wall appears above ground, though I was informed that they had been dug up at times and were three yards in breadth in some parts. The view is circumscribed but lovely, comprehending woody hills and the church tower. South of the Castle is a stream which no doubt fed the moat." *(Add. MS. 17, 458.)*

Ewyas Lacy Castle—see Longtown.

Frome Castle or Castle Frome.

———→•◆•←———

THE name of this place is so germane to the subject of our work that it is impossible to pass it over in silence, though we are bound to confess that the very existence of the fortress which once commanded the valley of the Frome is hard to establish.

There is upon the hill side within the limits of the parish, a grassy mound (called within the memory of man the Castle Tump) around which are some faint traces of a stream-fed moat, and in one ancient title deed (undated, but probably of the 12th or 13th century) certain lands are described as "infra ballivam castri de Froma Castri," *i.e.* within the bailiwick of the *Castle* of Castle Frome.

Our information as to the Lords of Castle Frome is happily much more extensive and has the advantage of being chiefly derived from the very curious and interesting series of title deeds in the possession of the Rev. William Poole, the owner of the manor.

Walter de Laci received for the services which he rendered to William I in the subjugation of Wales a grant of lands, in which was included a very large portion of the county of Hereford. As Ewyas or Longtown Castle was the head of the Barony we shall treat of the Lacies at greater length under that title. It may be sufficient here to observe that Castle Frome formed part of his possessions and, as such became in later times a member of the honour of Weobley ; in other words, it was held under the Lord of Weobley as the heir and representative of the Lacy family. *(see Weobley.)*

From the title deeds it appears that the mesne Lords of Castle Frome at an early date also bore the name of Lacy, but whether they were connected, legitimately, or illegitimately, with these more illustrious chiefs cannot be determined. Gilbert, Walter and Hugh were the prevalent Christian names in both families and it is quite possible that Dugdale may be inaccurate in some of the details which he gives of the Baron's descendants.

As a deed is extant in which Walter de Lacy grants to Stephen de Ebroicis lands in Frome Herbert and this deed is confirmed by letters patent from King John in 1205 *(see Appendix)*, we are able to obtain an accurate date from which to trace the subsequent descent of the lordship.

Walter's successor was one Adam de Lacy whose son Sir John de Lacy presented to the living in 1310. *(Swinfield's Roll.)* In the first year of Edward III (1327) Gilbert de Lacy was returned as holding the manor of the honour of Weobley according to the ancient feoffment. *(Lib. Scut.)* He granted it in 1341 to Sir William Devereux, knight, who had married Elizabeth, daughter of Richard Clodshalle, lord of the manor of Woodcote, county Worcester *(Title Deeds)*, and it would appear that some relationship existed between the Lacys and the Clodshalles. *(Pedigree of Unett)*.

Dame Elizabeth Devereux, after having married Sir Thomas Aston, knight, for her second husband, became again a widow. She was, however, attainted for felony, having been concerned in the murder of one Thomas Tidwyne, and her lands confiscated by Richard II. In 1386 the manor of Castle Frome was granted to Sir Simon de Burley *(see Appendix iii and Lyonshall)* but was subsequently restored to Dame Elizabeth and at her death divided between the two daughters of her first husband, viz., Margaret, wife of Richard Brace of Wiche, county Worcester, and Joane, the wife of James Hellions, of Westhide, county Hereford.

" The said Richard Brace by Margarett Devereux his wife hadd issue two daughters, Margarett Brace, wife to Robert Bromwiche, of Bromsborough, and Elizabeth Brace, married to John Unett. And James Helyon, by Joane Devereux his wife had issue two daughters, Margaret Helion, wife of John Muchgrose of Powick, and Agnes, married to William Monington, and the heire female of Muchgrose was married to Buck." *(Abstract of Title Deeds, written temp. Eliz.)*

The Unetts continued at Castle Frome, holding the lordship of the manor, for more than three centuries and intermarried with the Eltons, Nicholetts, Lingens of Stoke Edith, and other important families. The manor was purchased by the grandfather of the present proprietor, the Rev. William Poole, early in the present century, and he is now, with the Rev. John Hopton, the possessor of most of the parish.

74

Goodrich 1860

Goodrich 1860

Goodrich Castle.

——◆——

THE picturesque ruins of Goodrich Castle, on the summit of a red sandstone cliff which rises abruptly from the water's edge, are familiar to every tourist of the Wye, nor less familiar to every student of mediæval history are the names of the Castle's successive lords. In truth Goodrich is as rich in historical associations as it is in architectural beauties, and to neither subject can we do adequate justice in the few pages at our command.

There seems no reason to doubt that the nucleus of the fortress belongs to præ-Norman times and we may account for the absence of all mention of it in Domesday by the fact, which that record supplies, that all Archenfield had been ravaged and laid waste by the Welshmen Griffin and Blein, and consequently had not been minutely surveyed. To this Welsh incursion the Castle itself may have owed its origin, and there seems some probability in assigning the foundation to one Godric Mapsonne, who is mentioned as holding Hulla (*hodie* Howle) in the adjoining parish of Walford.

Within a century after the Conquest the Castle was in the hands of William Marshall, Earl of Pembroke (*Lib. Niger, i. 160*), whose possession of it, (derived perhaps through his wife the great heiress of the Clares who were lords of South Wales) was confirmed by King John in 1203. He held it by the service of two knights' fees—a service amply fulfilled by the life-long support which he rendered to his royal master against the insurgent

Barons.   Earl William was one of the most conspicuous personages of
his time   Eminent in the field, as his defeat of the barons at Lincoln
and his siege of London testify, he was equally distinguished by his sagacity
in the council—indeed he so won the confidence of his loyal peers that
they entrusted him with the guardianship of the youthful prince, Henry III.

He died in 1219 leaving five sons, all of whom succeeded in turns to the
earldom and died issueless.   His effigy in the Round Tower of the Temple
Church represents him as a warrior clad in chain-mail and surcote, with
legs straight and holding in his right hand the pommel of his sword, the
point of which pierces the head of the leopard on which his feet rest.
Beside him are the effigies of his eldest son William and of his third son,
Gilbert.   William was in his youth as stout an adherent of the baronial cause as
his father had been its opponent, but after his marriage with the daughter
of King John became allied in heart as well as in blood to the royal party ;
Gilbert, together with his brother Richard (whom Matthew Paris styles
" the flower of chivalry") were equally inimical to the king and their hostility
was adduced as a reason for refusing Walter, their younger brother,
livery of his inheritance.   Upon the death of Anselm Marshall, the
youngest of Earl William's sons and the tenant of the earldom for
eighteen days only, the vast possessions of the family devolved on his
sisters and co-heirs, the eldest of whom married Warin de Munchensi and
inherited Goodrich.   As their only son espoused the cause of the Barons
and fought on their side at Lewes, his lands became forfeited to the
Crown, and Goodrich was granted by Henry III in 1247 to William
de Valence, his own half-brother and the husband of the attainted baron's
only sister.   Dugdale relates some quaint stories about de Valence's lawless
doings in the neighbourhood of his castle at Hertford : how he poached in
the Bishop of Ely's park, broke open the prelate's manor-house, and
displayed his disgust at the smallness of the beer which he found
there by emptying the contents of the barrels upon the cellar floor.
His hands, however, were quite as apt for real war as for mischief.
He fought well at Lewes, and after that disastrous day fled to France,
from whence he returned to take part in the successful battle of Evesham,
and to reap the rewards which the reinstated king heaped upon his

adherents. He died in 1296 and was buried under a splendid monument in Westminster Abbey. His widow resided at Goodrich and we find her there in the year after her husband's death entertaining her friends in sumptuous style and feeding daily a score of poor neighbours. *(see Roll of Expenses, edited by Hartshorne.)* Among the guests was her son Adamar or Aymer de Valence who took an active part in opposing Piers Gaveston and in condemning Thomas, Earl of Lancaster, to death. He himself was murdered in 1323 while attending upon Queen Isabel in France, and his Castle of Goodrich then became the property of his niece Elizabeth Comyn, who carried it in dower to her husband, Richard, 2nd Baron Talbot. *(see Eccleswall.)*

Lord Talbot was summoned to Parliament from 1331 to 1355 by the title of " Richard Talbot of Goodrich Castle." He is thought to have expended a considerable part of the ransoms obtained from prisoners in the French wars on the improvement of the fortress, and Edward III granted to him and his wife (as they had almost sovereign power in Archinfield) " quod ipsi et heredes pro punitione malefactorum habeant domum carceralem infra castrum de Castro Goderici." *(Cal. Rot. Pat. 22 Edw. III.)* Richard Talbot was the founder of the adjoining Priory of Flanesford and dying in 1356 was succeeded by his eldest son, Gilbert, who served with the Black Prince in the wars of France. His grandson and eventual heir was Sir John Talbot, the first Earl of Shrewsbury, whose martial achievements are a matter of history. The hero of forty battles, foremost in the brilliant but profitless campaigns of the fifth and sixth Henry, he yet survived to the advanced age of eighty and was slain, sword in hand, at the battle of Châtillon in 1453. His son and successor met with the same fate at Northampton in 1460 and, as he was fighting in the ranks of the Lancastrian army, Goodrich reverted to the crown, and was granted by Edward IV to that zealous Yorkist, William Herbert, first Earl of Pembroke. *(Cal. Rot. Pat. 1 Edw. IV.)*

John, the third Earl of Shrewsbury, contrived to make his peace with the king and obtained from him the restoration of his estates, from which time until the seventeenth century Goodrich continued with his descendants.

It ceased, however, to be their principal seat, though we find it occupied
in Queen Elizabeth's reign by Gilbert Talbot (afterwards 7th Earl) during
the lifetime of his father and after his own marriage with Mary Cavendish,
the eccentric daughter of a still more eccentric mother. The letters
which passed between husband and wife are curious and incidentally afford
us information about the then products of the neighbourhood. " A
Monmouthe Cappe, a rundlette of Perrye, a payre of Rosse bootes" were
deemed no unfitting gifts to pass between a Countess and her lord.
(*Lodge's Illustrations.*)

On the death of Gilbert, 7th Earl of Shrewsbury in 1616 Goodrich
became the property of his daughter and co-heir Elizabeth, wife of Henry
Grey, Earl of Kent, and thirty years afterwards was the scene of one of
the most desperate sieges which took place in Herefordshire during the
Civil War. The fortress was at first in the hands of the Parliament, but
in 1646 was occupied by a garrison under the command of that eminent
loyalist, Sir Henry Lingen. Colonels Kyrle and Birch made a joint effort
to capture the Castle in the month of March, but only succeeded in
burning down the stables and out-houses and establishing a close blockade.
It soon became evident that the place could not be reduced by mere delay:
the castle was strong and well victualled and its defenders in good heart and
ably led. Birch had to procure fresh supplies of ammunition and more
powerful pieces of artillery before any effect could be produced, and it was only
when its numbers had been much reduced by successive sallies and the
powder and shot almost wholly expended, that the garrison was forced to
surrender. On the last day of July terms were proposed and accepted, by
which the lives and the honour of the brave defenders were preserved, and
four days afterwards Colonel Birch was permitted to take possession of the
battered fortress and the thirty barrels of beer which seem to have formed
its chief contents. Besides the Governor, Sir Henry Lingen, there were
fifty gentlemen within the Castle, whose names clearly shew to which
side in the struggle the chief families of the county were inclined.
The Pyes, the Lochards, the Bodenhams, the Wigmores, the Cornwalls,
the Vaughans and the Berringtons each and all had sent some member
of their houses to assist in retaining for the King this most important fortress.

On the 25th of August Parliament ordered Mr. Brown and Mr. Selden to acquaint the Countess of Kent of the necessity of demolishing the Castle, and early in the following spring it was finally resolved that it should be totally disgarrisoned and slighted. The ruins continued in the family of Grey, till the death of Henry, Duke of Kent in 1740, when they were sold to Vice-Admiral Thomas Griffin, one of whose granddaughters (widow of the late Major Charles Marriott of the Fort near Monmouth) still possesses them.

The Castle gave the title of Viscount to Henry, the first and last Duke of Kent of that creation, and this honour has by successive patents been permitted to descend to the senior representative of the family, the present Earl de Grey and Ripon.

Mr. King in his *Munimenta Antiqua* has described the fortress with careful minuteness, and though he is certainly wrong in assigning the keep to Saxon times, yet his other conclusions deserve the greatest respect. The general plan of the Castle was a parallelogram, flanked with round towers at the angles and surrounded on the land-ward side by a deep moat hewn out of the solid rock and spanned by a single drawbridge. The entrance, between two semi-circular towers near the east angle, was carried through a narrow vaulted passage 50 feet long, and defended at frequent intervals by a succession of gates and portcullises, and by rows of machicolations through which boiling water and molten lead could be poured down upon the assailants. Adjoining the entrance and running parallel with the passage on its left side was the Chapel, part of which was evidently constructed or restored so late as the reigns of Henry VI and VII, and close beside the chapel an octagonal tower which was used as a speculum. Of the angle-towers that at the south corner seems to have been occupied by the guard, and is so contrived as to give access from every part of the walls. Internally it is an irregular octagon and contained three stories in each of which was a fireplace. The great west tower is now in a very ruinous state though it is not earlier than the reign of Edward I, but the large fireplace which may still be traced suggests that the kitchen was in this part of the building. Between it and the north or ladies tower (which suffered greatly from Col. Birch's cannon) were the state apartments.   The hall, a noble room some sixty feet in length and nearly thirty in breadth, was lit with the trefoil-headed lancet windows of the early Edwardian era; its timbers (says *Silas Taylor*) were "of Irish oak and therefore untouched by spider or cobweb" and one of them "withoute knott or knarle sixty-six feet long and two feet square the whole length" survived till lately to testify to the character of the building.   "The hall communicated towards the north with a kind of withdrawing or retiring room, in which appears to have been a window looking into the hall : from the second apartment a passage led into what seems to have been the great state room which was 55 feet long and 20 broad.   At the upper end are two beautifully pointed arches, springing from a well-wrought octagon pillar in the middle of the apartment, and resting on corbels at the sides." (*Picturesque Antiq. of Hereford, p. 66.*)   The keep is of the usual Norman form—square with slightly projecting turrets at the angles.   It had three stories, access being gained by means of a newel staircase in the massive wall, and below the ground-floor was the dungeon "floored with Irish earth soe that whenever they brought a toade into it and layde it on the earthe it would dye." (*Harl. MS. 6726.*)   The keep was sometimes called Macbeth's tower, having formed (as tradition reports) the place of imprisonment of an Irish commander, by means of whose ransom the great Lord Shrewsbury was enabled to remodel the Castle.   It is certainly true that, whereas the other windows in the keep are evidently of the twelfth century, that in the middle apartment, which is said to have been the Earl's chamber, is of the style of Henry VI's reign.

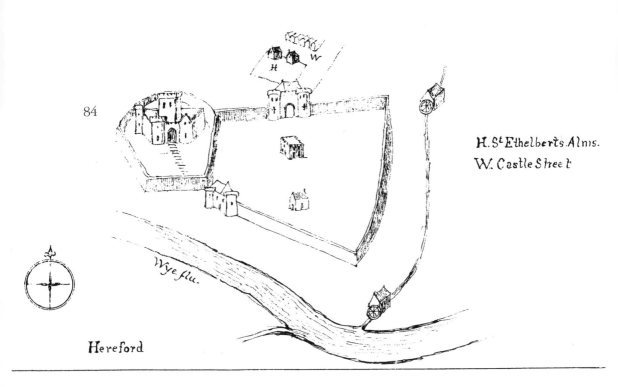

84

Hereford

Wye flu.

H. St Ethelberts Alms.
W. Castle Street

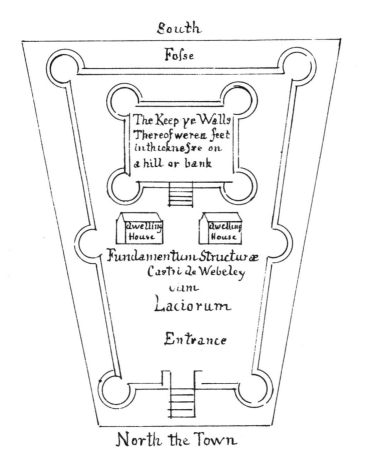

South

Fosse

The Keep ye Walls
Thereof were 2 feet
in thickneſse on
a hill or bank

Dwelling
House

Dwelling
House

Fundamentum Structuræ
Castri de Webeley
cum
Laciorum

Entrance

North the Town

Hereford Castle.

————◆◆◆————

It seems hard to believe that less than two centuries and a half ago there were still to be seen in Hereford the remains of a Castle which in circuit "was nearly as large as that of Windsor," and had evidently been "one of the fayrist, largest and strongest in all England." Such, however, is the testimony of Leland who describes its walls as being even in his time "high, very strong, and full of great towers," and no doubt much of the fortress must have survived till as late as the year 1746 when the site was converted into a public promenade.

It is not probable that any Castle existed at Hereford in Saxon times though there seems some ground to believe that Harold, after rescuing from the combined Welsh and Saxon insurgents the remnant of the town, caused it to be fortified with a wide trench and lofty rampart and perhaps raised the earthwork which subsequently formed the site of the keep. The construction of the actual Castle may without much hesitation be attributed to William Fitz Osberne, the first Earl of Hereford after the Norman invasion, and its government seems to have passed with the Earldom during the first century at least In the reign of Henry I, Milo, Constable of England and Earl of Hereford held the Castle in his custody for a time but on his espousing the cause of the Empress Maud, the Earldom and Castle were transferred by King Stephen to Robert de Bellamont, Earl of Leicester, who was the grandson of Roger de Bretevil, youngest son of William

Fitz Osberne.* The Empress in her brief triumph reappointed Milo to the Earldom, and by Charter, dated Oxford, AD. 1141, granted to him and his heirs the Castle of Hereford. Once more the tide of fortune turned and Milo, dispossessed of his honours by the return of King Stephen (who is said to have attacked the city in person), retired to the Abbey of Llanthony, near Gloucester and died a monk in the House which he had founded. It must have been under his orders that Geoffrey Talbot seized upon the city of Hereford and fortified its Castle and, according to some authorities, sustained there a siege by the Royal forces. *(Gesta Reg. Steph.* and *Matt. Paris.)*

Roger, the son and heir of Milo, had of course a strong claim upon the gratitude of Henry II which was acknowledged by a restoration of all his father's lost honours together with the "mote and whole castel of Hereford." These gifts, however, seem to have been insufficient to secure his loyalty. He joined Mortimer in refusing to obey the king's commands for the destruction of the numerous castles which had sprung up throughout England during the wars of Stephen and Maud, and established himself defiantly in his fortress at Hereford. Gilbert Foliot, the bishop of the see, has the credit of having reduced him to obedience and the king, having no confidence in the fidelity of any of the Barons of the Marches retained the Earldom in his own hands.

During the absence of Richard I in the Holy Land the Castle was entrusted to the care of Robert Bigod, second Earl of Norfolk, but he was displaced by the all-powerful Archbishop Hubert, who delivered the Castles of Hereford, Bridgnorth, and Ludlow "aliis custodibus custodienda ad opus regis." *(Roger de Hoveden p. 776.)* King John throughout the whole of his troubled reign was a frequent inmate of the Castle. We find him there as early as November 1200 and as late as the summer before his death, engaged on each and every occasion either in openly

---

* This grant is printed in extenso by Duncumb, *vol. i, p.* 232.

opposing the insurgent barons or in tampering with the Welsh with a view to procuring their support.

Except in particular emergencies the sheriff of the county was the usual custodian of the Castle. Thus in 1205 William de Cantilupe, (brother of the Bishop) held both these posts and though in 1215 when the Barons and Llywelyn were in open insurrection the Castle was committed to the custody of Hubert de Burgh, the grand justiciary, it was within a few weeks transferred to Walter de Clifford, the Sheriff, to fortify and hold,* and in the following year it was granted to Walter de Lacy, his successor in the shrievalty. Henry III was almost as frequently on the Welsh border as his father had been and the orders are numerous throughout his reign to store the Castle of Hereford, effect repairs, and increase its strength. For a time it formed the head quarters of the Baronial party and had Peter de Montfort for its governor, and it was hither that Prince Edward was brought after the battle of Lewes by his captor Simon de Montfort. His escape from confinement in 1265 on the horse which he was exercising on Widemarsh is an incident on which the old chroniclers loved to dwell and forms a prominent feature in in the most recent of historical dramas. *(E. L. Mitford's Prince Edward, London. 1869.)* Queen Isabella and her party met in Hereford and declared her son (afterwards Edward III) protector of the realm, and here the younger Despenser was hanged on a gallows in company with several of his adherents. After this time the Castle seems to have fallen into neglect. John of Gaunt, being governor in the time of Richard II, begged a store of timber from his neighbours for the repairs of the Castle, intending to have made it his chief abode, but the king deprived him of its custody, and the importance of the fortress declined rapidly after the pacification of the Welsh. When Leland visited it in 1520 the drawbridge was "cleane down and the whole castell tended towards ruine" though its form and extent were still plainly visible.

Stephen D'Evereux supplied the Castle with honey at the rate of thirty-two gallons a year, and Hugh de Clifford paid for the pannage of his pigs in Trivel wood by an annual contribution of bacon to the Castle larder. *(Close Rolls*, A.D., 1215.)*

In the Civil wars a portion of it, probably the keep, was fortified and garrisoned and no doubt the violence which was consequently directed against it helped to consummate its final destruction. A survey of it was made in 1652 after the death of King Charles and we gather from the particulars therein given that the outer baileys, including the Governor's lodge, were so ruinous as to be almost worthless. The space enclosed was five acres and a half: the annual value £6 10s. The keep was in better condition. The walls were strong and the tower had been covered with lead taken from the Chapter House ! The "old ruinous gatehouse" on the north side had been roofed by similar means, and there were still two ruinous houses within the Castle, one of which had been occupied by the main guard and the other for the common soldiers' quarters. An incidental statement shews that the castle had long been deserted. "A privilege of fishing in the river by reason of the discontinuance of inhabitants in the said Castle hath of a *long time* been discontinued." (*Duncumb, i. 286—288.*) Among the valuable collection of papers bequeathed by the late Mr. R. B. Phillipps to Belmont Priory is the conveyance of the Castle of Hereford by Colonel Birch to the County members. It states that Birch sold for £600 to Sir Robert Harley, Edward Harley, Walter Kyrle, Bennett Hoskins, Edmund Weaver and William Crowther, Esqs. "all that Scite Circuit and precinct of the ruinous Castle of Hereford, the waste land called Barbican adjoining to a certain mansion of the Cathedrall Church in which one John Green sometimes inhabited" &c. It further appears from this document that Charles I had granted the premises to Gilbert North, Esq., one of the gentlemen of the Privy Chamber, who had sold them to Edward Pye and others and they in turn had conveyed them to Birch.

The plan of the Castle is easily gathered from Leland's description and Speed's view. On the southern side the river Wye, the bank of which fell almost perpendicularly seven yards, formed a natural defence; and round the whole area of the Castle ran a semicircular wall defended with towers and strengthened with a wet moat "ubi non defenditur flumine." The entrance was on the north-eastern side over a great bridge of stone arches with a draw-bridge in the middle, and the eastern or outer bailey to which access was thus gained contained within it the chapel, the mill and the barracks and stabling. The smaller or inner ward had also a strong wall and deep moat and in it was situated the keep, built massively on a lofty artificial mound. It was from this side that attack was always most imminent, and hence the centre tower of the keep was raised high enough to command an extensive view and, if we understand Leland's words correctly, was strengthened at the base by no less than ten turrets.

The Treasury accounts contain many entries referring to the repairs and enlargement of the Castle, especially in the reign of Henry III. In the 17th year of that reign (1233) the sheriff of Hereford was ordered to construct at the head of the oriole of the king's chamber in the Castle "a certain fair and decent chapel, of the length of 25 feet" and to have the same wainscoated. *(Lib. Rolls.)* A chapel within the Castle must, however, have existed at an earlier period for we find that Earl Roger in the time of Henry II gave as a prebend to the church of Hereford "Capella Sci Martini in Castro Heref: scita"—*(Harl. MS. 6868)*. In the 26th of Henry III John le Werrur and Roger le Werrur, surveyors of the king's works and engines of war at Hereford, made oath that they had expended the sums of £7 8s. 6½d. in the workmanship of the said engines; £12 12s. 4d. in the construction of a certain trebuckett which was called "blithe," and £40 14s. 4d. in making a certain tower in the said Castle. *(Duncumb from Harl. MS. 7519.)* The oak with which the Castle was repaired was procured from the king's forest of Haywood and the stone supplied from the quarry there, but, in spite of the works, which till the reign of Edward III seem to have been constantly carried on, the buildings had become very ruinous at the close of the fourteenth century and did not subsequently undergo any general restoration.

It scarcely need be added that the ancient fortress now survives only in the names Castle Green, Castle Mill and Castle Street and that even the mound on which the keep once stood has been almost wholly levelled.

Huntington Castle,

WHICH stands on the extreme north western verge of the county, was included within the Marches of Wales until the year 1535, and from the very earliest times must have been an important position in that unsettled district. From the raised mound—the remnant of the original earthwork—the eye looks northward across the vale of Gladestry to the wild mountains of Radnor Forest, from whence has descended many a horde of Welsh marauders to ravage and lay waste the fertile fields of Herefordshire.

The date of the erection of the Castle is unknown, but we are inclined to think that it was much earlier than the reign of Henry III when we find it first mentioned. (*Cott. MS. Vesp. A. xviii.*) It was at that time in the possession of William de Braose, Lord of Brecknock, one of the staunchest adherents of the king against Llywelyn, but eventually the victim of the latter who suspected him of having an intrigue with his wife.

The honour of Brecknock, in which Huntington was included, devolved upon his widow Eva, sister of Richard Marshall, Earl of Pembroke, and at her death in 1248 it passed to their youngest child Elenor who had married Humphrey de Bohun, eldest son of the Earl of Hereford. De Bohun joined with Simon de Montfort and the other barons in their insurrection, though his father sided with the king. "In Feb. 1263-4 the Earl of Leicester's two sons, with a large force, wasted the territory of Roger de Mortimer and with the aid of Llewellin and his

Huntington 1847

Welsh forces took Mortimer's Castle of New Radnor. On hearing of these hostilities, Prince Edward marched hastily from London to Mortimer's succour : and having taken the castles of Hay, Huntington and Brecon, committed them with the adjoining country which belonged to Humphrey de Bohun to Mortimer's Castle, Humphrey de Bohun probably recovered possession of Huntington in July of the same year, when the Earl of Leicester reduced the Castles of Hereford, Hay and Ludlow, and wasted Mortimer's lands." *(R. W. Banks, Esq., Paper on the Manor of Huntington, Arch. Camb. 1869.)* But the royal cause though crushed by the disastrous defeat at Lewes, where de Bohun fought in the fore front, rose again the next year with the victory gained at Evesham. There de Bohun, recently honoured with the governorships of Goodrich and Winchester Castles, was once more a combatant and falling into the hands of the royalists was sent prisoner to Beeston Castle, where he soon afterwards died. Huntington Castle continued with the de Bohuns for four successive generations, each holder of the Earldom of Hereford occupying a distinguished place in the annals of his time. Humphrey de Bohun, the third Earl, by his marriage with Elizabeth Plantagenet daughter of Edward I, became closely allied to the blood royal and we find him at first fighting in the wars of Scotland on his brother-in-law's behalf and then joining with Thomas, Earl of Lancaster in the great insurrection which was raised to procure the banishment of the Despensers, It was from the Marches of Wales that de Bohun drew his forces, and every knight who held lands of the honour of Brecknock had to furnish his contingent and follow to the field his insurgent lord. In the battle of Boroughbridge, 16th March, 1321, the baronial party was defeated and de Bohun himself was run through the body with a lance and slain. His eldest son and successor died without issue in 1335, and as his second son never married, the earldom, upon the death of the latter, descended to Humphrey de Bohun, son and heir of William, Earl of Northampton, and nephew of the sixth Earl of Hereford. His tenure of the honours and vast accumulated wealth was very brief and at his death in 1372 his two daughters became his co-heirs : the elder of these married Thomas of Woodstock, Duke of Gloucester, sixth son of Edward III, and the younger became the wife of Henry Earl of Derby, who afterwards ascended the throne as Henry IV. The latter was created Duke of Hereford by Richard II, and Huntington Castle seems to have been his property until his accession to the throne, when the earldom of Hereford reverted to Edmund de Stafford, Earl of Buckingham, (who had married the only child of Thomas of Woodstock) and in 1399 he received an assignation of portion in all those knight's fees which belonged by inheritance to his wife's mother. He was slain at the battle of Shrewsbury, July 21, 1403, fighting for his king, and in the following September the custody of Huntington Castle (of which he had been seised) was committed to his widow. Owen Glendwr, encouraged by his defeat of Mortimer, was ravaging the Welsh Marches and if the Castle had hitherto escaped destruction at his hands, it could hardly be expected to be spared for long. The countess, therefore, "appointed John Smert, captain, constable of the Castle, who provided a supply of bows and arrows and employed a smith to clean the arms there. In October of the same year William Bourchier, Earl of Ewe in Normandy, (who a few years afterwards married the Countess) visited the Castle and stayed there with his family during the month, probably with a view to direct what was to be done for its defence and repair. The principal repairs during this year were re-roofing the keep with shingles and lead, rehanging with new hinges the great gate and postern gate, and the erection of palings by the *vivarium* and large barn : the making of a new fosse with a palisading on the same, from the Countess Tower to the grange." *(R. W. Banks, Esq. ut supra.)* Although the work of reparation seems to have been constantly going on, it was either inadequate or injudicious, for at the death of Humphry de Stafford, first Duke of Buckingham, in 1460 the Castle was returned as worth nothing *ultra reprisis.** It is, however, probable that it was in a habitable condition for at least a century afterwards and that the ill-fated Henry de Stafford the second Duke sought a refuge there when pursued by Richard III *(see Kinnersley.)* A survey of it was taken in 1521 when Edward the last Duke fell a victim to Wolsey's enmity and "the butcher's dog killed the finest buck in England." It had then fallen greatly to decay, though a tower was still employed as a

---

* Est ibidem quoddam castrum cum aliis edificiis quod nihil valet per ann. ultra reprisis. *(Inq. p.m.)*

prison and the office of constable continued. † The park was two miles in circuit, contained a hundred deer, and was in good condition. Blount states that in 1670 the keep was standing and most of the walls, and that the ruins indicated a Castle of large extent.

Such it evidently must have been to judge from the incidental notices of its various parts which Mr. Banks has discovered among the manorial account Rolls. "To the West and North it was protected by a steep ravine, and on the South and East it was within a moat supplied with water from a rivulet called Bellove. The outer walls formed an oval enclosure from North to South, of 75 yards and from East to West of 46 yards. The keep *(alta turris)*, which was roofed with shingles and lead, was probably on the East side of the raised mound. Other towers were called the Countess Tower, probably on the North East: and Reeve Tower, which last probably stood on one side of the great gate on the East   Within was the hall and a chamber to the North of it, a building styled the octagon, and a well. The entrance gate was approached by a drawbridge over the moat and a strong palisade, formed probably of wooden piles interlaced with flexible branches, extended along the counterscarp of the moat from the Countess Tower to the grange or great barn ......Traces of an outer court or outwork, which was probably fenced in by palisades or a hawthorn hedge, are still visible to the East of the Castle." *(R. W. Banks, Esq. ut supra.)*

After the attainder of the Duke of Buckingham the manor of Huntington, with the ruins of the Castle, went to the Crown and was granted in 1564 to Sir Ambrose Cave, Chancellor of the Duchy of Lancaster, for the sum of £6328 5s. od. Four years afterwards it was sold by Sir Ambrose to Francis Vaughan of Hargest and after passing through the hands of the Garnons, Townsend, Holman and other families *(see Kington)* it became the property in 1818 of Edmund Watkins Cheese, Esq. to whose representatives it still belongs.

---

† The survey mentions the other name of the Castle, viz., Castell Maen : *i.e.* the stone castle.

Kilpeck Castle.

◆·●·◆

THE scanty remains of Kilpeck Castle, once an important border fortress, are in striking contrast with the almost perfect condition of the co-eval Church which stands beside it. In the latter every stone, carved with a profusion of quaint ornament, attests the age to which it belongs, while of the former only a few massive fragments remain to mark the site and disappoint the antiquary.

Kilpeck, in Domesday Chipeete, was given by the conqueror to William Fitz Norman and there can be little doubt that the erection of a Castle there followed quickly upon the royal grant. Both Church * and Castle were in existence as early as 1124 *(25 Hen. I.)* when Hugh, the son of William Fitz Norman, gave to the Monastery of St. Peter at Gloucester the Church of St. David at Kilpeck together with the chapel of our Lady within the Castle. *(Chron. Sci. Petri. Glouc. in Bib. Cott.)* To this Hugh succeeded Henry, surnamed de Kilpeck, who had to pay a fine of 100 marks to King Stephen for trespassing in the royal forest of the Haywood and is represented in the Pipe Rolls of 1189 as owing an arrear of thirteen hawks which he ought to have furnished to the king from the forest of Trivel. *(Rot. Pip. 1 R. i.)*

The bailiship of the Haywood was granted by the Crown to John de Kilpeck, the son of Henry, who in 1193 purchased for £100 the

---

* The present church is dedicated to St. Mary. That referred to above belonged to the Priory of Black Monks which was suppressed in Bishop Spofford's time. 1422—1448.

Kilpeck 1837.

Barony of Purbech or Pulverbatch in Shropshire. He died 1204 leaving a son and heir under age and in the wardship of William de Cantilupe. His widow Juliane, gave the king 50 marks and a palfrey that she might have her dower and marry whom she pleased, but King John, who was a frequent visitor at Kilpeck Castle in the later years of his reign, pleaded the cause of her suitor, William Fitz Waryn in 1207 and induced her to accept him as her husband. *(Eyton's Salop.)* Hugh de Kilpeck, her son, on attaining his majority succeeded to the office of custodian of the royal forests in Herefordshire and is mentioned in 1248 as holding the manor of Little Taynton in Gloucestershire by the serjeancy of keeping the Haywood for the king. *(Placita, 32 H. iii.)* He left two daughters, his co-heiresses, the eldest of whom married Philip Marmion, hereditary champion of England and a staunch adherent of Henry III, and the younger, Isabella, became the wife of William de Waleraund, Sheriff of Wiltshire *(10 Rich. I)*, and had Kilpeck as part of her dower. Their eldest son Robert de Waleraund took an active part in the Barons' wars, fighting on the king's side at Evesham and holding for him the Castles of Cardigan and Carmarthen. We also find him in 1262 composing a difference which had arisen between the Bishop and Chapter and the citizens of Hereford relating to the assize of bread. *(Duncumb, 1, 300.)* By a deed dated 1269 he gave to his nephew, Alan de Plokenet (to the exclusion of the children of his brother William de Waleraund) the reversion of his Castle of Kilpeck, his park of Trevil and Coytmore; the forestership of the Hay with the manor of Hampton. *(Harl. MS. 5876. 6136.)*

Alan de Plokenet by virtue of this entail succeeded his uncle in 1272 and was summoned to Parliament as a Baron from 1295 to 1297. He was present at the battle of Evesham and distinguished himself in the Welsh wars, nor was he less eminent in other ways. By his skill a large portion of the Haywood, hitherto uncultivated, was redeemed and bears to this day the name of Alansmore, and the Abbey of Dore (where he was afterwards buried) was enriched by a grant of the advowson of Lugwardyne with the chapels of Hentland, Saint Weonards, Llangarren, and Little Dewchurch appertaining to it. He died in 1299 and was succeeded by his son of the same name, a combatant in the Scottish wars and in 1311 a Baron of Parliament. He obtained a charter for a weekly market and yearly fair at Kilpeck. On his death without issue in 1325 his sister Joan, wife of Edward de Bohun, became his heir, but, she also dying childless, Edward de Bohun, her husband, had license from Edward III to grant the manor of Kilpeck and Trivel and the Bailyship of the Haywood to James Butler, first Earl of Ormond, and Ellenor his wife, sister of the said Edward de Bohun. As the history of the Butler family belongs almost exclusively to Ireland it will be sufficient to mention that Kilpeck continued in their possession without interruption until the attainder of the fifth Earl, who was a devoted adherent of the Lancastrian party and after having fought at St. Albans and Wakefield was taken prisoner in the bloody battle of Towton Field 26th March 1467, and subsequently beheaded.

King Edward IV granted Kilpeck, which thus reverted to the Crown, to Sir William Herbert, first Earl of Pembroke, in reward of the many services he had rendered to the House of York. *(Cal. Rot. Pat., 4 6 Edw. IV.)* In 1469 he was taken prisoner in the struggle with the insurgents of the North at Edge-cote near Banbury, where his Welshmen were seized with panic and totally routed, and being carried to Northampton was there beheaded by George Duke of Clarence and Richard Nevil, Earl of Warwick who had recently deserted King Edward.

Kilpeck seems to have been restored to John, the sixth Earl of Ormond by Edward IV, who used to say of him, "that he was the goodliest knight he ever beheld, and the finest gentleman in Christendom." He died in the Holy Land on his way to Jerusalem and was succeeded by his brother Thomas, who was summoned as a Baron to the English Parliament by the title of Thomas Ormond de Rochford. His younger daughter and co-heir married Sir William Boleyn, K.B. the father of the Lady Anne, consort of Henry VIII, and the elder daughter brought Kilpeck in dower to her husband, James St. Leger. *(Originalia.)* His son and heir Sir George St. Leger was Lord of Kilpeck in 1545, but his family terminated in co-heiresses and early in the 17th century Kilpeck had passed to the Pyes of Saddlebow and the Mynde. Sir Walter Pye of the Mynde amassed an enormous fortune as Attorney General of the Court of Wards and Liveries in the reigns of James I and Charles I, not without suspicion of extortion. Contemporary gossip called him "the grandson of a Southwark butcher," but there is no foundation for the story, as he was in fact the descendant of an old Herefordshire family which had intermarried with the Kirles, Whitneys, Delaberes and Scudamores and had possessed the Mynde for four generations. Sir Walter's son and heir, of the same name, was probably the wealthiest landowner in the county. Symonds says that his father's income was £25,000 per annum and his property included the Mynde and "Kilpeck Castle—the last decayed, a parke about it now." Young Sir Walter was on the side of the king throughout the Civil war and was sent by the besieged as their hostage when Hereford surrendered to Colonel Birch. He died in 1659, too soon to see the Restoration of the house of Stuart for whose sake he had sacrificed his fortune, and his son Walter, who clung with equal devotion to the same unhappy dynasty, received from the hands of James II after his abdication the empty title of "Baron Kilpeck." The Castle then consisted only of bare walls and though during the Parliamentary struggle it had been occupied by a garrison and in 1645 was "slighted" *i.e.* dismantled *(Symonds's Diary. p. 212)*, it is described by Leland as ruinous even in his time. *(Itin. 86 b.)*

Kilpeck was purchased with other property by Richard Symons citizen of London, about the year 1740 and descended eventually to his sister's issue. The late T. G. Symons of the Mynde parted with it in exchange to the Rev. Archer Clive some ten years ago.

All that now remains are a few fragments of the keep, the walls of which are about six feet in thickness, rising straight for three or four feet and then sloping inwards, buttress fashion, and again ascending in their first form. They enclosed a space from 70 to 80 yards in diameter, and in this a deep well was recently discovered. These two fragments, ragged and ivy-grown, were perhaps portions of slightly projecting turrets, for in both a semi-circular fireplace may be traced.

The situation of the Castle is very striking. A lofty mound, very steep
on the north-eastern side and encircled by two wide ditches, commands
the valley through which the river Worme pursues its tortuous
course, and a background of wonderful beauty is formed by the Black
Mountains and the more varied shapes of the Sugar Loaf and Skerrid
hills. Separated from the Castle mound by the grass-grown moat
is the curious Norman Church—itself a cabinet of exquisite sculpture,
which though it does not come within the scope of our work to notice at
any length, we may commend to the careful attention of the antiquary
and ecclesiologist.

Kingsland Castle.

―――→•◦●◦•←―――

LELAND, writing about the year 1529, says "There was a Castle at Kingsland, the ditches whereof and part of the keepe be yet seen by the W. part of Kingsland Church. Constant fayme sayth that King Merwald sometymes lay at this place; since, of later times, it longed to the Earl of March, now to the King." The existence of the Castle was therefore something more than a tradition in the sixteenth century and if by the word "keepe" we are to understand the remains of stonework we must refer its construction to a much later period than that of the Saxon Prince Merewald, who founded Leominster Priory about the year 660.

Indications of an extensive building have been traced from time to time within the garden of the Rectory, and spear and arrow heads found buried in the Mound, but no mention can be discovered in the Public Records of any castle at Kingsland. Possibly the Mortimers, who were owners of the manor and benefactors to the Church, might have erected upon Saxon foundations some sort of fortified residence, but it is hardly probable that it could have been of any importance in the fifteenth century, otherwise it would have been mentioned in connection with the frequent struggles of that period and with the great battle between the houses of York and Lancaster which was fought within the parish in 1460 and known in history as the battle of Mortimer's Cross.

It should be added that the meadow adjoining the Castle and asserted have been the burial place of the Saxon king, still bears the name of "Merwold Croft."

Kington Castle

RESTS upon almost as unsatisfactory a basis as Kingsland Castle. We have indeed the name of Castle Hill, still existing, to indicate the position of the fortress on the northern side of the Church, but Mr. Parry, the historian of Kington, was unable to discover any record of the building or to suggest a date for its erection or decay.

Mr. R. W. Banks, with better success, has found among the manorial papers a note respecting the rent paid in 1529 for "the pasture of the Castle Hill and *of the moat of the same Castle* and also for the farm of the fishpool and one pasture about the Castle, of old belonging to the porter of the same Castle" : and he further remarks that "the Castle Hill till the middle of the last century, formed part of the demesne lands : but there is no spring or course by which the pool or moat could have been supplied with water." It is, however, not necessary to suppose that the moat was a *wet* ditch, and we are inclined to believe that from very early times a mound, encircled by a deep trench existed at this spot and that subsequently a tower was erected upon it for the double purpose of watching the approach of the enemy and of sheltering the neighbours from the frequent inroads of Welsh marauders.

The borough of Kington is included within the manor of Huntington and has, until very recent times, descended with it. As has been already stated *(p. 95)* the manor was sold by Queen Elizabeth in 1564 for

£1,328 5s. 11d. to Sir Ambrose Cave, Chancellor of the Duchy of Lancaster, and an intimate friend of Lord Burleigh. A story is told of him that at a court ball he had the good luck to pick up Her Majesty's garter which had slipped off as she was dancing, and on the Queen refusing to accept it he tied it on his left arm and vowed he would wear it for his mistress's sake as long as he lived. The maiden Queen was not indifferent to such gallant speeches and perhaps some of Sir Ambrose's success in life may be due to his tact on this occasion.

He disposed of the manor of Huntington two years afterwards to Francis Vaughan of Hargest, a descendant of the hero of Agincourt whom we have already mentioned *(see Bredwardine)*. His grandson sold it again in 1583 to John Garnons, a member of an ancient family whose name is still commemorated in their original dwelling place, now the seat of Sir Henry Cotterell, Bart. Thomas Garnons parted with Huntington and Kington in 1616 to Sir John Townsend from whom they were purchased five years afterwards by Sir Samuel Tryon, Bart. (the opulent son of an emigrant from the Low Countries) and Philip Holman, Esq., who eventually became possessed of both moieties and built the market house at Kington. The son of the latter was created a Baronet in 1663 and his eventual co-heirs, Mary, wife of Thomas Eyre, Esq., and Ann, Countess of Stafford sold their interest to Edward Greenly Esq., of Doctors' Commons in 1749. From Edward Greenly, jun., the property was purchased by John Harris of Brilley, whose heirs were the family of Cheese. A division of the property took place in 1840 when James Cheese of Kington, reserving to himself the Castle of Huntington, disposed of the Kington property to James Thomas Woodhouse of Leominster. *(Parry's Hist. of Kington.)* The manor has been still further subdivided and is now in the hands of numerous proprietors.

Kinnersley Castle.

The name of Kinnersley contains in it the earliest history of the place. Some Saxon colonist, called Kynard or Kynworth, made his clearing *(ley)* in the dense forest which covered the greater portion of Western Herefordshire, and in the fosse and stockade, raised to protect him from the attack of man and beast, laid the foundation of the future Castle. At what period the stone structure was first erected it is impossible to say as every trace of it has been effaced by the comparatively modern building which now occupies its site, but supposing it to have been coeval with the tower of the Church, we should assign it to the reign of Henry I. It formed at an early period the home of a family which took its name from their place of residence and the old pedigree of the Kinnersleys or Kynardesleys is adorned with the representation of a moated Castle (of a very conventional type) in front of which stands an old man, halberd in hand and supported by twelve armed men, awaiting the passage across the drawbridge of three mounted soldiers. The preamble of the pedigree informs us that this represents John de Kynardsley and his son receiving the sheriff and his officers when they came by the Conqueror's order to survey the land for the Doomsday book! The further information (of a less questionable character perhaps) which the same authority furnishes, is that "the armes ye Kynnardsleys bore at first was Azure a Lyon rampant argent, untill one Hugh de Kynardsley went into ye Holy Land with Prince Edward in vita H. 3. where he received knighthood and had ye Hierusalem Crosses added to his Coate of Armes."

Kinnersley

For ourselves we can only state that one Hugh de Kynardesley was Sheriff of Herefordshire in 1250 and that while in the discharge of his office he was taken ill, whereupon Robert de Trillet, clerk, and Reginald de Rode were appointed to adjust and pass his accounts. (*Mem. Scacc. 35. Hen. III. Rot. 17: Duncumb. i. 348.*) From the Monasticon we further learn that he was a benefactor to the Abbey of Craswall, and his name occurs in the list of knights serving under Edward I. In the first year of the reign of Edward III Richard de Kynardesley is returned as holding one hide of land in Kynardesley for half a knight's fee by military service of Symon de Burley, of whom we shall have more to say as sometime lord of Lyonshall. (*Lib. Scut.*) Kynardesley was a member of the great "honour" of Wigmore, and of course its mesne lords had to furnish their quota of armed retainers to follow their suzerains, the Mortimers, to the battle field. John de Kynardesley occurs in 1316 as lord of Newchurch (a township in the parish), and in 1318 received pardon for having joined in the rebellion of Thomas, Earl of Lancaster. (*Parl. Writs.*) The last of the family of whom we find mention are John de Kynardesley and Matilda his wife who presented to the Parish Church in 1335 and 1339. (*Episc. Reg.*) Their heiress, (either sister or daughter) married Richard de la Bere who in right of his wife became Lord of Kinnersley and obtained in 1340 license to hold a market and fair there. He served as Knight of the Shire in 1355 and won his spurs at the battle of Crecy. Dying in 1382 he was buried, together with his widow Sibilla, in the Monastery of the Black Friars at Hereford. His son, named Kynard to commemorate his mother's family, presented to the Church of Kynnersley in 1382 and from his designation "nobilis vir" we may infer was also advanced to the dignity of knighthood, and from this time forward the name of de la Bere becomes one of the most prominent in the annals of the County and matched with its most important families.

The chief historical interest which attaches both to the house of de la Bere and the Castle of Kinnersley is derived from an incident in the life of the unfortunate Henry Stafford, Duke of Buckingham, of which we are able to give the details which a contemporary MS. has preserved.*

It will be remembered that among the powerful nobles who helped Richard III to seize the Crown one of the most active was the Duke of Buckingham, a man in whose veins no little of the royal blood of England ran. Whether there arose in his mind a natural reaction when he saw the evil results which attended his too successful exertions and remorse led him to seek their reversal cannot be determined with certainty, but it is evident that the Duke, in spite of the honours heaped upon him, early conceived a hatred against the hand that bestowed them. Archbishop Morton, a zealous Lancastrian, directed his attention to the young Earl of Richmond, as the only person who could free the nation from Richard's tyranny and accordingly the Duke raised in his favour the standard of revolt in the Welsh Marches where his own influence was predominant. (see *Huntington.*) His designs, however, were rendered abortive partly by the floods which made the Severn impassable, and partly by the hesitation displayed by the Courtenays and other fellow conspirators. The Duke therefore "came from Brecknoke to Webblie and with him brought my Ladie his wife, my Lorde Stafforde and my Lorde Henrie and there tarried one weeke and send for the gentlemen of the countrie unto him, and when he had spoken with them departed thens and at his departing delivered his Sonne and Heyre to Sir Richard Delabere knight for to kepe until he sent for him by a token." Most faithfully did both Sir Richard and his wife Elizabeth fulfil this trust, concealing the youthful family of the Duke at Kinnersley and thus averting from them the same bloody fate which involved their father. (*See Appendix iii.*)

There can be no question of the authenticity of the narrative subjoined and of course, if it be true, the statement of Fuller falls to the ground

---

* The original roll, (which, we believe has never been published) was found among the evidences at Thornbury Castle, Gloucestershire, a magnificent seat built or rather commenced by Edward, last Duke of Buckingham.

that Richard de la Bere was knighted on the battle field of Stoke (1487). The de la Beres retained possession of Kinnersley until the reign of Elizabeth* when Sanacre de la Bere, brother and heir of Sir Thomas, gave it in dower with his daughter Elizabeth to Richard, son of Sir Michael Lyster, Knt. By him it was sold to Francis Smallman, a cadet of the Elton family of that name, who, after serving as M.P. for Leominster in 1620, died at Kinnersley in 1633. His son, by his second marriage, succeeded him and married a daughter of that gallant cavalier Sir Robert Whitney, who, surviving her husband, remarried John Booth of Letton, "an old Royalist and a zealous lover of the Church of England." (*Mon. Ins. in Cathedral.*) Kinnersley passed with Lucy elder daughter and co-heiress of William Smallman to her husband, James Pytts of Kyre co. Worcester. He sold it about the year 1660 to Sir Thomas Morgan, knight (created a Baronet 1 Feb. 1660-1), a member of an old Herefordshire family seated at Vowchurch in the Golden Valley, and distinguished as one of the most successful parliamentary officers in the West of England. Major General Morgan stood high in the favour of Monk who committed to his charge the custody of the Castles of Edinburgh and Leith and the command of the Army when he went southwards to prepare the way for the restoration of Charles II; and it was in recognition of his important military services that the dignity of a Baronet and the governorship of the Island of Jersey were subsequently conferred upon him. His son and successor was sometime governor of Chester Castle and M.P. for the county and at his death in 1689 left issue (besides a son who succeeded

*The de la Beres were Lords of Tibberton till late in the 16th century when Kynard de la Bere sold it to Will. Brydges, Esq. with whose eventual heiress Mr. Lee-Warner obtained it in marriage. Southam near Cheltenham (now the seat of Lord Ellenborough) was also the property of the de la Beres and there is still preserved a very curious picture representing a knight kneeling on a cushion and holding in his hand a helmet which has just received the crest—a plume of five ostrich feathers issuing out of a ducal coronet. The constant tradition has been that this picture (certainly a very ancient one) commemorates a distinction conferred by Edward the Black Prince upon Sir Richard de la Bere who rescued him from imminent peril in the battle of Crecy (1346).

A daughter of the above Kynard Delabere married Richard Perks of Drayton and in the Pritchett family, who derive from this marriage, the name of Delabere has been perpetuated to the present day.

him in the estates and representation of the county) two daughters, the elder of whom married John Walsham, Esq., of Knill Court (ancestor of the present Sir John James Walsham, Bart.) and the younger became the wife of Thomas Clutton of Pensax co. Worcester, to whose children Price, James, and Henry Clutton in succession, Kinnersley was bequeathed by their cousin the last Baronet. Thomas Clutton Esq., of Pensax sold Kinnersley in 1801 to Leonard Parkinson, Esq. whose daughter and heir married in 1812 J. A. Graham Clarke, Esq. of Newcastle-on-Tyne. From Mr. Clarke the Castle and Manor were purchased by Thomas Reavely, Esq., their present possessor, some ten years ago.

No view of the mediæval Castle of Kinnersley is extant and the Elizabethan building which occupies its site has wholly obliterated all traces of it. From time to time foundations have been discovered below the soil which seem to indicate that it was a quadrangular structure, encircled by a moat which was spanned on the eastern or park side by a drawbridge.

NOTE—Mr. Wright, in his *History of Ludlow*, (*pp.* 150—1) seems inclined to identify the Castle of Kynardslegh which in 1223 was given to Baldwin de Hodnet with Kinnersley in Herefordshire; but the writ conveying the king's order to that effect was addressed to the Sheriff of *Shropshire* and it is therefore more probable that the place indicated is Kinnerley in that county. Mr. Eyton, the historian of Salop, has discovered at Kinnerley traces of an ancient castle, though he confesses his inability to shew Baldwin de Hodnet's right to it or to any other Kinnerley. (*Hist. XI.* 23.) On the other hand, the events in connection with which the above grant was made seem rather to favour Mr. Wright's opinion and we shall therefore leave the matter with our readers, only adding a brief recital of the incidents to which we have referred. On July 6, 1223, the king, being then at Worcester, orders the sheriff of Shropshire to give Baldwin de Hodnet immediate and full seisin of the Castle of Kinardslegh, and a contemporary writ orders a similar restoration of Whittington Castle to Fulk Fitzwarin. (Whittington Castle had been beseiged by Llywelyn in the preceding February). On the same day the king issued other writs prohibiting all intercourse with Llywelyn, who within the next two months took Kinnersley Castle by storm and proceeded to lay siege to Reg. de Braose's Castle of Builth. King Henry mustered his army at Gloucester and advanced by way of Hereford and Leominster to Montgomery, Llywelyn meanwhile having been excommunicated as a truce-breaker. These measures brought the Welsh prince to terms and on October 7th Llywelyn was absolved and swore to satisfy the king for all damages done by the Welsh to the English since the capture of Kinnersley Castle. That Castle, on the 9th of October was, by the king's orders, restored to de Hodnet and the Sheriff was commanded to give him full seisin of his land of Kinnersley. (*Close Rolls.*)

Lingen Castle

WAS less important as a fortress than as the seat of one of the most ancient Herefordshire families, which derived its name from the little village of Lingen on the borders of Shropshire. The Mortimers were the chief lords of the entire district and under them one Turstin held the manor of Lingen at the time of the Domesday Survey. From that record we gain some further information about this Turstin whom genealogists affirm to have been ancestor of the Herefordshire Lingens. He was usually styled Turstin de Wigmore, no doubt from the fact that he held lands in that Chatellany, and with his wife Agnes, daughter of Alured de Merleberge *(see Ewyas Harold)*, he obtained the lordship of Great Cowarne. His descendant, Ralph de Wigmore, Lord of Lingen in the reign of Richard I, was founder of the Priory of Lyngbroke or Limebrook, which Leland erroneously attributes to one of the Mortimers, and there can be no reasonable doubt that Lingen became the patronymic of his family from thenceforth. In the fortieth year of Henry III (1256) Sir John de Lingen had a grant of free warren for himself and his heirs in Lingen, and four years afterwards was one of the dictators on the king's part of the truce between him and Llywelyn—the king empowering him to settle the terms of amend which the Prince of Wales was to pay. *(Blount's MS. Rymer's Fœdera.)* Sir John's daughter Constantia married in 1253 Grimbald, son and heir of Sir Richard Pauncefort, and had for her dower 630 marks, twelve beeves, and one hundred sheep, besides the manor of Great Cowarne. *(Blount's MS.)* The story of her devotion to her husband is better known than attested.

Grimbald joined in the crusade against the Mahommedans of Tunis and was taken prisoner by them. His captors demanded a joint of his wife—whose beauty perhaps had been a subject of boast—as the price of his ransom and tradition adds that the terms were accepted and the lady's left hand procured him his release. Silas Taylor gives the following account of the monument erected to the memory of the devoted pair in the south aisle of Cowarne Church. " I diligently viewed the accord which might have been between the two figures : the female laid next the wall of the south aisle on her right side by which means his left side might be contiguous to her right, the better to answer the figure : also, the stump of the woman's arm is somewhat elevated, as if to attract notice ; and the hand and wrist, cut off, are carved close to his left side, with the right hand on his armour, as if for note." Whether the mutilated effigy and the lady's name, Constantia, are the sole foundations on which this story of heroic love rests we will not presume to say.

Another John de Lingen, probably the son of Sir John, is stated to have been knighted by Edward the First " at a great solemnity in order to a Royal voyage against the Scots " in 1306. (*Ashmole's Hist. of the Garter.*) A century later Richard de Lingen, second son of Ralph de Lingen was entrusted with certain powers—(their nature Blount was unable to ascertain)—by which on behalf of the king he granted permission to Janin de Brompton to buy and sell cattle in Herefordshire and the adjoining Marches for his own use and profit, "sans refreshment des rebelles de Gales" *sc.* without benefit to the insurgents under Owen Glendwr.

In the reign of Edward IV the name of Lingen appears for the first time in the List of the Sheriffs of Herefordshire. Sir John Lingen, who served that office in 1470 and 1476 added greatly to the importance of his family by marrying one of the co-heirs of Sir John Burgh. He lies buried with his wife in Aymestry Church and the beautiful brass upon their tomb has hitherto been fortunate enough to escape the hands of the restorer and the collector. Sir John Lingen's son, a knight of the same name, acquired Stoke Edith by his marriage with Eleanor, heiress of Sir

Thomas Mildwater, and dying in 1530 was succeeded by a third Sir John who married Margaret, daughter of Sir Thomas Englefield of Englefield co. Berks, sometime Speaker of the House of Commons. Their eldest son John Lingen of Sutton left an only child, Jane, who was born in 1544 and, influenced perhaps by her cousin Sir Francis Englefield who lost his estates and his liberty by opposing the Reformation, was a warm supporter of the old religion. Her husband William Shelley of Michaelgrove co. Sussex was a no less ardent Romanist and suffered attainder in 1583. Butler says that his only crime was petitioning Queen Elizabeth for a mitigation of the laws against the Roman Catholics in consequence of the loyalty they had displayed at the time of the Spanish Armada; but the account given in the Records is very different. The indictment charged Shelley with having imagined and compassed the death of the Queen, the subversion of the established religion and government and the procurement of an invasion of the kingdom, and evidence was adduced to prove a traitorous interview with Charles Paget, an outlaw and friend of the Earl of Northumberland. *(Baga de Secretis, p. 47.)* Shelley was found guilty and committed to the Tower, but though subsequently sentenced to death, he seems to have ended his days in the Marshalsea prison. Nor did his wife escape similar severity. "Parsons, in his reply to King James, dilating on the sufferings of the Roman Catholics, mentions Mrs. Shelley as a gentlewoman of good worship cast into the common gaol of Worcester, for that a priest was found in her house." *(Blakeway's Sheriffs of Salop.)* At her death in 1610, Radbrook in Gloucestershire passed to Sir Richard Preston, Lord Dingwall, "one of the herd of hungry Scots that swarmed in the court of James I," but Sutton and other Herefordshire estates went to her cousin Edward Lingen. The manor of Lingen was granted by King James to Sir John Peyton, junior, nor was it ever afterwards restored to the Lingen family, though they were distinguished for their loyalty throughout the Civil War. John Lingen, a captain in the king's service was slain at Ledbury and his elder brother Sir Henry we have had occasion already to mention. *(Brampton Brian, Goodrich, &c.)* He was one of the chief Royalists in the county and received the honour of knighthood from King Charles's hand in 1645 "at Mr. Prichard's house near Grosmont."

(Symonds's Diary, 205.) His losses were proportionate to his services. The fine levied by Parliament upon his estates amounted to £6342, and his property had been heavily taxed by the maintenance of a regiment of horse. He lived to see the Restoration and died of small pox at Gloucester on his way home from London where he had been attending the House of Commons as M.P. for his native county. By his wife Alice, daughter of Sir Walter Pye, he had two sons and fifteen daughters but only two of this numerous family had issue, viz. Frances who married John Unett and Alice wife of Herbert Herring. On them devolved the estate of Sutton, but Stoke was sold under the will of Sir Henry's son to Paul Foley, Esq., and is still enjoyed by the widow of his descendant, Lady Emily Foley.

Mr. Evelyn Shirley admits into his *Libro d'Oro*—"the Noble and Gentle Men of England"—Robert Burton, Esq. of Longnor, as the representative of the Lingens of Radbrook, who abandoned their patronymic in 1748; but more than one branch of the old tree still survives and the present Secretary to the Committee of Council, Ralph R. W. Lingen, Esq., is the direct descendant of Thomas Lingen of Leighton Court (younger brother of the loyal knight) by his wife, Catherine, daughter of Matt. Meysey of Shakenhurst. We believe also that Charles Lingen, M.D., of Hereford claims a share in the representation of the Radbrook branch, so that there is no chance of the name of Lingen being soon forgotten.

118

Longtown 1864

Longtown Castle

WAS in earlier times designated Ewyas Lacy Castle, as the chief fortress in the Hundred of that name, and the original seat of the Lacy family in the Marches of Wales. It is also sometimes called Clodock Castle from its situation in that district.

There seems little doubt that the Romans had occupied the site for military purposes and possibly left materials enough for William Fitzosborne, the first Norman Earl of Hereford, to construct therewith a border fortress, which passed from his hands to those of Walter de Lacy, the hero of Hastings and the lord of West Herefordshire. Walter died on March 27, 1085, from injuries received in a fall while superintending the building of St. Peter's Church at Hereford. His son Roger de Lacy, who was Lord of Ewyas at the time of the Domesday Survey, rebelled against Rufus and was banished in 1095, when his forfeited estates were conferred upon his brother Hugh de Lacy who died childless early in the 12th century. About the year 1143 Gilbert de Lacy, nephew of the deceased baron, (being his *sister's son*), was recognised by Stephen as lord of Ewyas and as he had lost his Norman fief by transferring his allegiance from the Empress Maud to the usurper, the latter compensated him by conferring on him his uncle's English estates. Like many another warrior in those times, he grew tired of constant fighting and before his death assumed the Templars' habit and retired from the world. Of his son and successor Robert * (whom Dugdale altogether omits) we know little, but

---

* A letter from Gilbert Foliot, Bishop of Hereford (in the Register of the Dean and Chapter of Hereford) states that in his time the service performed for Hom Lacy by Gilbert de Lacy, and afterwards by his successor *Robert* was the service of two knights.

his brother Hugh de Lacy II obtained from Henry II a charter confirming Ewyas and other estates to him, and he accompanied that king in his expedition to Ireland in 1172. Their progress throughout the island was one of triumph and when Henry returned home "he gave to Hugh de Lacy the whole of the lands of Meath with all their appurtenances, to hold in fee to himself and his heirs by a hundred knights' service, and also left in his custody the city of Dublin, appointing him Justiciary of Ireland." *(Hoveden, i. 354.)* Being summoned to help his king against Prince Henry who was plotting treason with Louis VII in France, he won high honour by his gallant defence of Verneuil, but on returning to Ireland incurred the king's displeasure by marrying, without the royal licence, a daughter of the Prince of Connaught. There was also a suspicion that Lacy intended to found an independent kingdom for himself in Ireland and his estates were therefore escheated and he himself assassinated at Durrow in 1185. Four years after his father's death Walter de Lacy, the eldest son, recovered possession of the forfeited lands and some notion of the vast extent of his Norman fief may be gathered from the fact that the escheator had received from it in the previous year £750 in money, besides produce in kind—grain, wine, and fish. *(Rot. Scacc. Norm.)*

The history of Walter de Lacy's career is full of incident and interest. His rebellion in Ireland was quelled by King John with summary severity. Lacy and his brother were outlawed and his mother-in-law Matilda de Braose and her eldest son starved to death in the dungeons of Windsor Castle. Yet five years afterwards, in 1215, Walter de Lacy had recovered possession of his estates on payment of an enormous fine and was thenceforth, to all appearance, loyally attached to his king. In 1216 Margaret de Lacy, Walter's wife founded the religious house at Aconbury wherein prayer was to be made for her many relatives who had been victims of John's former cruelty. Throughout the reign of Henry III Walter de Lacy remained true to his king, defending the English rights in Ireland even in opposition to his own brother, Hugh, the lord of Ulster. At length, worn out with suffering and blind from old age, Walter died in 1241, and his possessions became divided between his two granddaughters and co-heiresses, the younger of whom married John de Verdon who thus acquired the Castle of Longtown.

De Verdon had summons as a baron marcher, and adhered to the side of the king in his struggle with the nobles. He subsequently accompanied Prince Edward to the Holy Land as a crusader and died in 1274. Ewyas Lacy then devolved on his son Theobald who for a while was under the displeasure of Edward I for treason and other misdemeanours, but was restored to favour on his submission and the payment of a heavy fine, "the king taking into consideration the good services of his ancestors." At his death in 1309 he was succeeded by his only son of the same name, who for some time was governor of Ireland and, for his first wife, married one of the daughters of Edmund Mortimer, Lord of Wigmore. He had no male issue, and on the division of his estates in 1316 Ewyas Lacy became the property of his second daughter Elizabeth, who married Bartholomew de Burghersh, one of the most distinguished warriors in the reign of Edward III. His son of the same name and of equal reputation with himself fought beside him at Crecy, and at a very early age, and during the zenith of his father's military fame, was made a Knight of the Garter. At Poictiers he captured the renowned Baudouin d' Ennequin and at Courmicy made the governor a prisoner by sapping the principal tower of the fort. After filling many important offices he died in 1369 leaving an only daughter Elizabeth, who married Edward Lord le Despencer, who had fought beside him at Poictiers and with himself was one of the founders of the Order of the Garter. Their son was the celebrated Thomas le Despencer, Earl of Gloucester, who matched with the blood royal and adhering too closely to the fortunes of the weak Richard II, lost his life and his lands to no purpose.

His only daughter Isabel married Richard Beauchamp, Lord Abergavenny, whose heiress became the wife of Edward Nevil (son of Ralph, Earl of Westmoreland) and conveyed to him the Baronies of Burghersh and Abergavenny. In the latter of these he was summoned to Parliament in 1450 and Longtown Castle, which had descended through the line which we have traced, thus became the property of the Nevilles, Lords Abergavenny, in which family it still remains.

The Castle, which is said to have surrendered to a Welsh army under Howell, Prince of North Wales in 1146, (*Powell's Hist. of Wales*), has evidently been from the earliest times a position of much military importance. Mr. Bodley, the architect, considers that the keep was built prior to the Conquest and there can be little doubt that the site had been continuously occupied for military purposes from the time of the Romans, who established there a strongly entrenched camp, till the Wars of the Roses. "An outer wall, composed of mould and stones raised at least to the height of 20ft., enclosed about a hundred yards square, in the N.W. angle of which, on a keep somewhat higher than the wall, stood a circular tower, of which the greater portion remains, having three round buttresses or turrets at equal distances and between these as many circular apertures for windows." (*Murray's Handbook.*) Near the top of the keep is a projecting latrine, very curious and perfect, and over one of the windows of late insertion some roses have been carved. Access to the inner court was obtained through an arched gateway defended by a portcullis the groove of which is still visible, and strengthened by circular pillars on either side of large proportions. The grey tower of the keep stands out in bold relief against the dark background of the Black Mountains and the air of lonely wildness which pervades the scene makes it a fitting retreat for the *genius loci* who has elsewhere been banished by the advancing tide of civilization.

124

Lyonshall 1869

Lyonshall Castle.

————→●◆●←————

THE name Lyonshall has undergone a surprising number of mutations and is not found in its present form till late in the seventeenth century. Lenehalle, (as it was then termed,) formed at the time of the Domesday Survey part of the possessions of Roger de Lacy and had belonged to Earl Harold in the reign of the Confessor. At an early period, in all probability during the eleventh century, it was occupied under the Lacies by a branch of the family of d'Ebroicis or Devereux, the descendants of which became in after time its chief lords.

Much confusion exists in all the printed accounts of the Devereux family and the fact that there were at least three contemporary lines resident in Herefordshire and often bearing the same names seems to have been ignored by every genealogist. Of the two earliest members of the Lyonshall branch we know very little. William and his wife Helewysa were benefactors to the Abbey of Gloucester in the reign of William Rufus, and their successor Walter held three knights' fees of Hugh de Lacy in 1165. *(Lib. Niger Scacc.)* Twenty years afterwards John d'Ebroicis gave to the knights of St. John of Jerusalem the Church of Oxenhall in Gloucestershire, of which place his descendants at Lyonshall continued to be Lords for a long period. His successor was Stephen d'Ebroicis and either he or a son of the same name is mentioned in 1209 in a letter from Walter de Lacy to King John, wherein Lacy says that he has received the Castle of Lenhaul from Stephen d'Ebroicis in custody for the King, *(Pat. Rolls, p. 90),* and we further learn from various writs that Stephen adhered to

King John in his contest with the Barons and accompanied him in his expedition to Poitou in 1214. Stephen married Isabella de Cantelowe (who subsequently became the wife of Ralph de Pembrugge) and was the chief founder of the Priory of Pyon, or, as it was afterwards called, Wormsley. His letter to the Bishop of Hereford appropriating the Church of Lyonshall to the Canons of Pyon is quoted at length by Blount. In it he grants to the Priory "the whole Church of Leonhals, reserving a reasonable endowment for the Vicarage" *(salva rationabili Vicaria)* and expresses his regret that the urgency of his affairs prevents him from tendering his gift in person. This grant was subsequently confirmed by the Bishop and the Dean and Chapter of Hereford, the former claiming for himself the right to assess the Vicar's portion and to augment or diminish it according to circumstances. The Vicar was to give constant personal attendance to his parish and was allowed to have the Rectory House together with a pasture called Parson's Croft. *(Deed dated Sugwas, vi. Cal. Apr. A.D. MCCC xiiij.)* Stephen d'Ebroicis was succeeded either by his son or brother William, who had summons in 42 Henry III to attend the king at Chester with horse and arms to restrain the incursion of the Welsh; and Prince Edward also in 1263 begs his father to command Will d'Evereus "quod in castro suo de Le Hales (*sc.* Lyonshall Castle) moram faciet ac partes suas viriliter defendat." *(Fœdera, 47 H. iii.)* He continued loyal until the battle of Lewes when he forsook the royal standard and afterwards fell fighting on the side of the barons at Evesham. His widow, sister of Walter Giffard, Bishop of Bath and Wells, recovered by the king's permission the jewels and harness which he had deposited in the Cathedral of Hereford, but his lands became forfeit to the crown and were granted to Roger Mortimer of Wigmore. By the payment of 100 marcs William Devereux, the son, had Lyonshall Castle restored to him *(Placita)*, and by his wife Lucia had issue a son, John, who predeceased him. Stephen Devereux, the son of John, claimed to possess certain rights over the property even during the lifetime of his grandfather William, and from the legal proceedings which were taken we learn that William Devereux granted the Castle and Manor of Lyonshall to Roger la Warre for his (William's) life and Roger granted it to Walter de Langton, Bishop of Lichfield for the same term and the Bishop being thus in seisin alienated it in fee to William Touchet and Maria his wife. A verdict therefore was given in 1301 in favour of Touchet because, William Devereux * being still alive, no claim on the part of Stephen had arisen. *(Plac. de Juratis et Assizis, 29 Ed. I.)*

There seems little doubt that William Touchet (who was summoned to Parliament from 28 Edw. I until 34 Edw. I) made Lyonshall Castle his chief seat, for to the famous letter to Pope Boniface in defence of the rights of the king he subscribed his name as "Lord of Leuenhales," and obtained a charter for a market there every week and a yearly fair at Michaelmas. He took an active part in the Gascon expedition and Scottish wars and died early in the reign of Edward II. Whether Lyonshall became forfeited to the crown through the treason of his son or passed from the family by some other means does not appear, but it is mentioned as one of the manors of which Bartholomew de Badlesmere, "a great Baron and as great a Rebel," was seised at his execution in 1322. As his only son Giles de Badlesmere died without issue, Lyonshall became the property of his eldest sister and co-heir Maud, who married John de Vere, seventh Earl of Oxford, one of the heroes of Crecy and a commander upon the glorious field of Poictiers. *(Dugdale's Bar.)* It was certainly in the possession of his son Thomas, eighth Earl, in 1371 † and probably descended to Robert, the 9th Earl of Oxford and 1st Duke of Ireland. The career of that haughty favourite of the weak king Richard II is full of romantic interest; and there must have been something noble and endearing in the man who could so retain the affections of a vacillating prince that the truest mourner at his funeral

---

* The Lord of Lenhales, Sir Wm. Devereux, had incurred excommunication for having detained the tithes of his manors, but he disregarded it. The Bishop, therefore, wrote to the king's justiciaries not to admit him to appear as plaintiff till he had made satisfaction to God and the Church for his offence. This produced effect and his absolution was formally pronounced at Bosbury 7 Nov., 1290. *(Swinfield's Roll.)*

† Thomas de Vere, Earl of Oxford and Matilda his wife, plts., and Nicholas Gernon, chivaler, William de Wyngefeld, chivaler, John de Horsham, clerk, Walter de Wotton and John de Haukwode, sen., deforc. of the Castle and Manor of Leonals with appurtenances. *(Fines, 45 Edw. III, No. 80, Record Office.)*

was the monarch whose love he seemed to have spurned and whose confidence he had abused. Some time before his death in 1392 Lyonshall had been transferred to another royal favourite Sir Simon de Burley, K.G., whose family derived their name and origin from the little village of Burley, near Leominster, which they held under their superior lords, the Mortimers. Sir Simon is said to have been introduced at court by his learned kinsman Walter de Burley, and to have commenced his chivalrous career at the age of fourteen by serving in the fleet which destroyed the Spanish corsairs in 1350. From that date until 1369, when to the grief of his master, the Black Prince, he was captured at Poitou, he was incessantly in arms and he reaped the reward of his prowess so soon as his former pupil, Richard II, ascended the throne. He became successively governor of Windsor and Llanstephan Castles, Master of the Falconry and Keeper of the Royal Mews, and was enriched with divers manors and estates. In 1384 he had licence to imprison thieves and robbers in his Castle of "Lennolx" *(Rot. Turr. 8 Ric. II)*, and soon afterwards reached the culminating point in his life. Either the envy of the Duke of Gloucester or his own arrogant conduct proved his ruin. He was charged with treason and though the king offered to answer for his innocence and knelt with the queen to supplicate his pardon, the duke was inexorable and Burley was condemned to death on the 15th May, 1388.

Two years afterwards the king granted Lyonshall to Sir John Devereux, a descendant of its former possessors and husband to Margaret, the daughter of John de Vere, Earl of Oxford (by Maud Badlesmere). He succeeded Burley not only at Lyonshall, but in his stall as Knight of the Garter and in his offices of Constable of Dover Castle and Warden of the Cinque Ports. At his death in 1393 he left an only son, who died unmarried, and a daughter, who thus became his eventual heiress. She married Walter, fifth Baron Fitz Walter, who in 1403 had orders from the king to fortify his Castle of "Lynhales" against the Welsh insurgents under Owen Glendwr. *(Rymer, viii. 328.)*

Some partition of the Devereux estates must have occurred about this period, and thus Lyonshall fell to the share of Agnes Devereux (widow of Sir Walter Devereux a kinsman to Lady Fitzwalter) who was the wife of

John Merbury in 1418.*   At any rate we find that ten years afterwards, viz.,
6 Hen., VI, John Merbury held one fee in Lyonshall formerly the Lord
Fitzwalter's. *(Dugdale, Bar. 176.)*

Merbury, who was sometime Chamberlain of South Wales and a
personal attendant of Henry V, who left him £100, had issue an only
daughter who became the wife of her cousin Sir Walter Devereux, and
thus conveyed Lyonshall once more into that family.   There it continued
for two centuries *(see Weobley)* until the death of Robert Devereux,
third Earl of Essex in 1641 without male issue, when it descended to his
eldest daughter Frances, eventually Duchess of Somerset.   She died in 1674
bequeathing her property to Thomas Thynne, afterwards Viscount
Weymouth, who had married her granddaughter, and Lyonshall was sold by
their descendant Thomas, 3rd Viscount Weymouth and 1st Marquis of
Bath to John Cheese, Esq., whose representatives still possess the Castle site.

It would appear that the Castle ceased to be occupied as a residence after
the beginning of the fifteenth century, probably on account of damage inflicted
upon it by Welsh marauders and the gradual progress of decay.   Leland says
there was in his time a park about it, but late in the following century Blount
describes it in these terms:—"It seems to have been a noble structure, but now
nothing remains of it but the old walls."

At the present time it is not difficult to trace the form and extent
of the ancient Castle, for the two moats, both filled with water, still
exist and the walls of the inner bailey are in some parts tolerably perfect.
These walls enclosed a space some sixty yards in diameter and appear
to have formed an irregular heptagon or octagon with a turret at each
angle.   On the north side of the bailey was the keep, circular in shape
and about twelve yards in diameter at the present base.   It was entered
by a flight of steps from the south side and in the ruined walls may still be
traced three or four deeply splayed embrasures.   It should be noticed that in
this instance, as in so many others, the Castle stood contiguous to the Church
as though to defend it from harm, but that the latter has survived its protector.

* John Merbury and Agnes Devereux presented his wife to Ludlow Church 5 Hen. V.
(Wright's Ludlow.)

Moccas Castle.

◆·•·◆

We are enabled by means of the Public Records not only to assign a precise date to the foundation of Moccas Castle, but also to form some sort of notion of the nature of the building. In the year 1291 Hugh de Fraxino or de Frene, (a descendant of one Walter del Freisne who held lands in the honour of Kington of Adam de Port in 1165) obtained a charter of free-warren in his lands at Moccas and Sutton and three years afterwards had a royal license from Edward I to fortify his manor house at Moccas "and to strengthen it with a stone wall without tower or turret and not exceeding ten feet in height below the battlements." *(Rot. Pat. 21 Edw. I.)* Whether these limitations were not adhered to or the works had been prematurely began does not appear, but on the 4th April in the same regnal year Hugh de Frene was summoned to appear and show cause why he had erected a castle or fortified house at Moccas without the king's licence and the Sheriff of Hereford was directed to seize it on behalf of the king. *(Memoranda Roll 21 Edw. I. MS. 22.)* The dispute was probably settled by a fine and the de Frenes remained in undisturbed possession of Moccas.

In the 10 Edw. III Hugh de Frene (of the same family with the above) had summons to Parliament as a baron of the realm, but only in that year. This Hugh is presumed to be he who married Alice, daughter and heir of Henry de Lacy, Earl of Lincoln and widow, first, of Thomas, Earl of Lancaster and secondly of Enbolo le Strange; in right of which lady, he is said to have claimed the Earldom of Lincoln. The last of the de Frenes whom we find in connection with Moccas was Richard Frene, chivaler, who died seised of it about the year 1375,* when his heirs were declared to be the three sisters of his father Richard, viz. Alice, the wife of Roger Criketot : Margaret, the wife of Sir John Joce and Elizabeth the wife of John Talbot of Snayington. *(Inq. p.m. 49 Edw. III.)* Roger Cricketot seems to have succeeded to Moccas as his name occurs in the Episcopal Registers as patron to the Church, but in the early part of the reign of Henry VI Moccas belonged to Edw. ap Meredyth. *(Lib. Scut.)*

We have already mentioned Moccas in connection with the Vaughan family *(see Bredwardine)* and from Fines and Inquisitions we learn that it was their property at least as far back as the reign of Philip and Mary. Tradition avers that it went from them in the following manner. Henry Vaughan of Moccas, Esq. married (at Much Dewchurch) in 1635 Frances one of the daughters of Sir Walter Pye. She was left a widow and continuing to reside at Moccas with her son Roger, found a second husband in a young man who was caught hunting deer in the park. The story goes that she was so much struck with the prisoner's appearance that she not only forgave the offence but permitted him to condone it by marriage with herself— a result which is rendered less surprising by the fact that the poacher was a cadet of the ancient family of Cornewall of Berington *(see Stapleton)* and may not improbably have intended his shaft for nobler game than ranged the Park.

Her son by her second marriage not only succeeded to Moccas but acquired the rest of the Vaughan property.

"At the restoration Henry, son of Edward Cornewall of Moccas" (the husband of Mrs. Vaughan) "was made Page of Honour to the Duke of York. He was not 14 when he went on board the same ship with H.R.H. to Holland where he formed an acquaintance † which in process of time enabled him to purchase Bredwardine, adding the Weston to it ; and his mother lived to see a son by a second husband in possession of a better estate than her eldest son had squandered in drunkenness, &c." *(From a MS. letter addressed to Catherine, daughter of Velters Cornewall, penes Sir G. H. C.)*

* A mailed effigy in Moccas Church "by his face but young," is assigned by Silas Taylor to a member of the Frene family, probably to the above.

† No doubt this refers to Henry Cornewall's first wife, Marita Laurentia Huyssen, of Middleburgh in Zeeland. He married, secondly, Susannah, daughter of Sir John Williams, Bart., of Pengethley

We cannot do more than mention two eminent members of the Cornewall family whose names are not yet forgotten in Herefordshire, viz. Velters Cornewall who was M.P. for the county during seven successive Parliaments, and his younger brother James, who by his gallantry in the naval action before Toulon in 1744 won for himself the nation's gratitude and a tomb in Westminster Abbey. The heiress of Velters Cornewall by his third wife Catharine Hanbury married Sir George Amyand, Bart. whose descendants assumed the name of Cornewall and are represented by the present Baronet, the Rev. Sir G. H. Cornewall.

The site of the ancient Castle may be readily traced in a meadow, lying on the south side of the high road east of the park. The foundations have long formed a quarry for road metal, the moat, partially drained, is now only a swampy circle and a few grassy hillocks alone mark the spot on which the old buildings stood. The later residences of the lords of Moccas have been nearer the river and probably closely contiguous to the modern mansion. Silas Taylor *(Harl. MS. 6726)*, who was himself nearly related to the Vaughans, says "there be large trenches about ye howse and neare to it with a mount over ye river Wye yet to be seen." These traces have now disappeared but possibly indicated the residence of " King Drabeles, alias Pibianus, king of Irchunfeld," whose tomb—" raised two feet from the ground of the purest coloured marble, being perfect green, white, yellow, and black in exact proportions of rounds,"—Taylor saw within the Church. *(Ibid.)*

Mortimer's Castle.

———◆•◦•◆———

It has been already stated that the parish of Much Marcle possessed at an early period two baronial residences *(see Ellingham)*. One of these, as is indicated by the name, was occupied by the Mortimer family, a portion of Much Marcle (Blount says two thirds) having been granted to Edmund de Mortimer by King Edward I in recognition of important services. The grandson of Edmund was the ambitious Roger de Mortimer, whose intrigues with Queen Isabella and the part he took in the murder of her husband have procured for him a bad eminence in the history of his country. He was hanged in 1330, and his body is generally supposed to have been conveyed from the Grey Friars in Smithfield, where it was first buried, to Wigmore the seat of his ancestors. Blount, however (following perhaps some well-founded tradition) asserts that the stone monument in Marcle Church with its two effigies was erected in memory of Roger de Mortimer and his wife Joane, daughter of Peter de Genevil, and that the former is there interred.* As there are no arms or inscriptions upon the tomb to help in deciding the point, we must leave the subject with the remark that there are several known instances of duplicate monuments being raised in commemoration of the same individual. *(See Herald and Genealogist, vol. I.)*

* Blount is clearly wrong in assigning the other (alabaster) monument to " Lady Blanch, daughter of Roger Mortimer, 3rd Earl of March and wife of John, Lord Audley." In the first place it was *Joane* Mortimer who married *James*, Lord Audley ; and in the next place the arms of Grandison and Mortimer on the monument rather favour the supposition that the monument commemorates Lady Blanch, daughter of Roger Mortimer and wife of Sir Peter de Grandison.

The last Earl of March devised his share of Marcle to Thomas Walwyn *
for life, (*Blount's MS.*), and out of the ruins of the Castle was constructed
the tower of the church "wch is not of a meane forme." *(Harl. MS. 6726.)*
On the accession of Edward IV, the heir of the Mortimers, this portion of
the manor returned to the crown and was purchased in the reign of Queen
Elizabeth by Thomas Kyrle of Walford, a scion of a family which produced
two such eminent but widely discordant members as John Kyrle, the loyal
" Man of Ross" and his kinsman the rebel Colonel, one of Cromwell's most
active officers. *(See Goodrich and Hereford.)*

The son of the purchaser was created a baronet in 1627 and his eventual
heiress, Vincentia Kyrle, married Sir John Ernle, Knt., and conveyed Marcle
to her husband.   Their son, John Kyrle Ernle, had an only daughter
Constantia, who, having no issue by her husband Viscount Dupplin, settled
her estates on her kinsman and heir James Money, son of Francis Money of
Wellingborough by Elizabeth Washbourne, granddaughter of Sir John Ernle.
A baronetcy was a second time conferred on the family at the queen's
coronation in 1838, but the first baronet, Major-General Sir John Money,
who assumed the additional name of Kyrle, died without issue and thus
the title became extinct, but the estates passed to his younger brother
the Rev. William Money Kyrle, whose third surviving son is their
present possessor.   In the 17th century the site of the Castle near the
church and the moat around it could be clearly traced *(Harl. MS. 6726)*,
but are now almost effaced.

---

* Thomas Walwayne de Marcle Ar. tenuit die quo obiit Man. de Magna Marcle cum
ptin. de Dno Rege ut de Castro suo de Wiggemore per fidelitatem et red. xviii s. per ann.
(Inq. p.m. 7 Edw. IV.)

Pembridge 1846

COWELLS ANASTATIC PRESS, IPSWICH

138

Pembridge 1846

Cowells Anastatic Press Ipswich.

Pembridge Castle.

———→•◄———

THERE seems much reason for believing that in this instance the usual process of nomenclature has been reversed and that the Castle owes its name to its original founder. The family of Pembridge or Penebrugge were lords of the town of that name as early as the reign of Henry I and continued to reside there even after the chief lordship had been transferred to the Mortimers. *(Blount's MS. ; Eyton's Salop.)* At the beginning of the 13th century Ralph de Pembridge was settled at Welsh Newton on the confines of Monmouthshire, and perhaps to show his connection with the ancient family of which he was a scion gave to his residence the designation of Pembridge's Castle. It does not appear to have been attached in any way to the manor of Pembridge, on the contrary it was from an early period a member of the manor of Newland in Gloucestershire, though held of the honour of Wigmore.

Ralph de Pembridge died before 1219, as in that year we find William de Cantilupe impleaded Reginald de Braos for the custody of his heir. He lost his cause as Reginald showed that he had not the custody of the heir at the time the writ was taken, but that Henry de Pembridge had it. *(Coram Rege Roll, 3, 4, H. III.)*

We are unable to say what relationship existed between Ralph and Henry de Pembridge, nor can we with any certainty identify the latter with the active partisan of Simon de Montfort who, after setting fire to Warwick, was captured by Roger de Mortimer and imprisoned in Wigmore Castle. There were in fact several branches of the Pembridge family, the main line being that which was seated at Tong Castle, co. Salop, and the most important branches in Herefordshire being those of Clehonger and Mansel Gamage.   The Pembridges of Newland and Clehonger seem to have been one and the same family.   Henry de Pembridge, sen., who had lands in Clehonger (*Placita de Jur. et Ass. 13, Edw. I*), passed the manor of Newland by fine to Henry de Pembridge, jun., and it was subsequently settled, in case of failure of issue, on his brother Richard.   *(Hereford Fines.)* This Richard succeeded him and founded a chantry at Clehonger, 15 Edw. III. *(Inq. ad quod Damnum.)*   He seems to have died before 1346, in which year his widow Petronilla had licence for an oratory at Clehonger.   Their son Richard was the gallant Knight of the Garter whose monument is a conspicuous ornament in Hereford Cathedral.   He is first mentioned as forming one of the staff of Edward III on his landing at La Hogue in 1346 ; he was probably present at Crecy and the siege of Calais and was certainly among the most renowned English knights who fought at Poictiers. In 1361 he obtained a grant of the custody of Southampton Castle and manor and of the New Forest for life, and in subsequent years he filled many public offices and was honoured with the Governorship of Bamborough Castle and the Wardenship of the Cinque Ports.   In 1368 he was elected a Knight of the Garter and shortly afterwards was appointed Chamberlain of the Household.   His career suffered in 1373 by his refusal to act as the king's deputy in Ireland and many of the grants which had been made to him by royal favour were revoked. *(Beltz's Garter.)*   Still he retained a large portion of the lands with which he had been enriched and died seised of them on 26th of July, 1375.   He was buried in Hereford Cathedral, and the helmet, tabard, and shield suspended above his monument were to be seen in the last century when Gough engraved them for his *Monumental Effigies.* The two latter have been stolen and the helmet was purchased by the late Sir Samuel Meyrick and added to the armoury of Goodrich Court.

Sir Richard left an only child, Henry, who was 15 years old at his father's death and died on the first of October following, his heirs being Sir Richard Burley and Sir Thomas Barre, the children of Sir Richard's two married sisters. *(Esc. 49 Edw. III.)*

Newland, including Pembridge Castle, fell to the share of Burley, a name which we have already had occasion to mention *(see Lyonshall).* Sir Richard Burley who thus succeeded to Pembridge was, like his father Sir John * (the husband of Amicia Pembrugge) and his uncle Sir Simon, a Knight of the Garter, and vied with them in the glory of his military achievements. At the battle of Auray in 1364 he had command of the van and especially distinguished himself in the memorable engagement in which the constable Du Guesclin was made prisoner and Charles de Blois slain. Early in 1382 he was elected a K.G. and five years afterwards, on the 12th of May, exhausted by the disease which had almost destroyed the English army in Spain, he expired at Vilhalpando in the province of Leon. *(Beltz's Garter.)*

In old St. Paul's there was a splendid monument to his memory erected probably by his wife Beatrice who founded in the cathedral a chantry for the repose of the souls of her husband, his father and mother, Sir Richard de Pembridge, and others. As he left no issue his estates devolved on his brother William who also died *s.p.* in 1388. Roger Burley, his next brother succeeded him, upon the failure of whose issue in 1445 the manor of Burley and other lands of the family devolved to Thomas Hopton, as his cousin and next heir, he being the direct descendant of Sir John Hopton who had married Isabella, only daughter of Sir John Burley. Newland, however (together with Pembridge Castle), was in the hands of Thomas Beaufort, Duke of Exeter and third son of John of Gaunt, at his death in 1427, when he is stated to have held it of Richard, Duke of York under age and in custody of the king, and of the honour of Wigmore. † *(Esch. 5 Hen. VI.)* In the next century it belonged to the Baynham family and became a subject of litigation between the executors of William Baynham, Esq., and the Aubreys of Clehonger. *(Chanc. Proc. temp. Eliz.)*

---

* A distinguished soldier and ambassador in the reign of Edward III and Richard II, elected K.G. and made keeper of Sherwood Forest in 1377. He died about the year 1383 and was buried in the Church of the Black Friars at Hereford.

† Gough, (in his additions to Camden) states that in the reign of Hen. VII it was held by the Knights Hospitallers of Dynmore, and afterwards by Margaret, Countess of Richmond and Derby. She certainly died seised of it but perhaps, as the mother of Henry VII, had a grant of it.

After passing through the hands of one David Baker it was sold to Sir Walter Pye, Knt., and formed during the Civil war an outpost to the royalist garrison of Monmouth, suffering severely in the campaign of 1644. "The news of the taking of Monmouth reached Col. Massie near Burford prosecuting the commands of the Committee of both kingdoms ... hence he makes haste to the relief of the party sent out against Chepstow ... and at Gloucester understood that it was safely landed on this side Wye, having effected nothing. The Governor met them in the forest and thence marched to Rosse where he hoped to have passed the bridge to the relief of Pembridge Castle, which was made an outguard to the garrison of Monmouth, but found the bridge broken down and the river made impassable by the sinking of boats on the other side and a guard of horse to defend it. Here we had some disputes with the enemy for two days and those in the Castle, having no means of a further subsistence, were enforced to surrender upon quarter and the freedom of their persons; most of the common soldiers revolted, being formerly of the King's army and our prisoners." (*Corbet's Military Govt. of Gloucester. Bibl. Glouc. p.* 128.)

From Sir Walter Pye, junr., the Castle was purchased by George Kemble, gent., who repaired the ruins and rendered the place habitable. In this state it has continued ever since. Henry Scudamore, gent., was its occupant in 1715 and it afterwards belonged to the Townleys of Lancashire, by whom it was sold to the late Sir Joseph Bailey, Bart., father of the present owner, whose tenant farms the ancient park and demesne.

The fortress is in a comparatively perfect condition, and is a quadrangular structure about 45 yards from north to south and 35 from east to west. The entrance is on the south side, defended by two towers of unequal size, the smaller one standing on the south-east angle of the enclosure. Access to the court-yard is gained through a dark vaulted passage 33 feet long, in which two, if not three, gates may be traced with machicolations between them and the grooves of the portcullises. The drawbridge, which when drawn up filled exactly the space between the entrance towers, no longer exists, and this part of the moat is now filled up and rendered solid. In the courtyard at the left side a door between two square-headed windows leads to what, judging from the size of the fireplace, was the kitchen. Adjoining this at the south-west angle is the keep tower the basement of which is used as a cellar and the three floors above it have wholly disappeared. The farmer's kitchen and parlour were once the great hall and the staircase in the projecting square turret formed of solid blocks of oak is undoubtedly original.   The north-west angle is supported by a very singular turret-like circular buttress about 7ft. in diameter, which has perhaps been a campanile to the castle chapel.   The tower at the opposite angle is even more curious. The ground plan is a quarter of a circle of 11ft. radius with straight sides projecting at right angles from the north and east respectively seven feet. This structure was carried up above the roof ridge of the adjoining buildings and possibly was used as a watch tower.   The loop-holes in the north curtain wall were evidently made at the time of Massie's siege, and these are the only features in the building to which we can assign an unquestionable date.   *(See Mr. Wakeman's Monograph on Pembridge Castle in the Cambrian Journal.)*

From the Rev. J. Webb's MSS.—

(Pembridge Castle had passed from the knightly family of Pembruge to the Pyes of the Mynde in the 17th century.)

"Sir Walter Pie by Indenture dated Sept. 20, 6° Caroli granted the Castle and lands for 99 years to George Kemble, Gent. Ann, his wife, and Richard, their son, who afterwards mortgaged it to Charles Wilford, of London, Gent. by Indenture dated May 22, 1640, and Wilford entered into the premises for non-performance of the covenants of the said Indenture, 18 March, 1650, and assigned the same unto Richard Reeve, of Farley Wallopp in the county of Southampton, Gent.   In 1650 George Kemble being dead one year, the premises were sequestered for recusancy of Anne Kemble his widow : but upon representation of the case the Commissioners were satisfied of the just claim of Reeve, and discharged the sequestration accordingly." *(State Papers, Ser. I, vol. LIII, folio 305.)*

The Castle was recovered by Col. Kyrle after the recapture of Monmouth and seems to have held out in the first instance for a fortnight until provisions failed.

Penyard Castle.

——→•◦•←——

PENYARD, "the hill enclosure," stands in accordance with its name high upon the wooded hill-side above the village of Weston near Ross, and was well fitted for the defence of the narrow pass through the woods from Gloucestershire towards the counties of Monmouth and Pembroke. The fortress was of no great extent, but there are still some fragments of massive walls and groined arches to be seen, and in the last century "in digging among the ruins a kind of vestibule or spacious passage was found with octagon pilasters, which have caps and bases in the Saxon style, from which spring semi-circular groined arches with handsome mouldings in sharp preservation." *(Bonner's Itinerary, ii, 15; Beauties of England and Wales, vi, 516.)* This description is not very lucid, but we may perhaps gather from it that the fragments exhumed were the remains of a Norman or early-English chapel attached to the Castle.*

Penyard belonged to the Talbots as early as the 13th century, and probably formed a part of the original grant made to the family in Herefordshire *(see Eccleswall).*

The position of the Castle, commanding an extensive prospect, and yet surrounded by a dense and tangled wood, would give it favour in

* There is among Ministers' Accounts at the State Paper Office, the fragment of a note respecting the repair of Penyard in 11 Edw. III.

the eyes of a feudal lord who divided his time between the chase and the sterner field of war. Even in the 15th century, when both Goodrich and Eccleswall had been in a measure deserted by the family, we find Sir Lewis Talbot, a younger son of the great Earl of Shrewsbury, seated at Penyard. It continued with his descendants till the death of Gilbert, 7th earl, in 1626, when it devolved upon his second daughter, Elizabeth, Countess of Kent * and was sold, together with the adjoining property, in 1740. Mr. Partridge, of Bishopwood, was the owner of the site at the beginning of the present century, and it now belongs to the Rev. H. Usborne of Bitterne.

There seems to have been a mint established at the Castle in the sixteenth century and silver pennies of a particular coinage have occasionally been found there. Guillim states that the family of Spence of Hangwest co. Ebor bore for their arms, *circa* 1638, "azure, three Penyard pence, proper." We cannot find that the family was connected with the place, and probably these bearings were assumed solely on account of the punning allusion contained in them.

---

* Among the State Papers is a petition, dated 20th Oct., 1631, from Henry, Earl of Kent and Elizabeth, his wife, begging that Sir John Kirle, of Much Marcle, to whom Penyard Park had been leased, might be restrained from felling the timber-trees. These, amounting to 20,000, had been reserved by the lease, but notwithstanding Sir John "has felled and converted into coal for making iron above 1,800 trees and still continues."

Richard's Castle.

---•◆•---

N the Domesday Survey of Herefordshire mention is made of a Castle called Auretone in Catesthorne Hundred which was worth 20s. per ann. to Osbern Fitz Richard and wherein he had 23 men who paid him half the said income, and again that a manor within the Chattelany of Auretone was held in the time of the Confessor by one Richard. Mr. Eyton, the historian of Salop, conjectures with much probability that this Richard was Richard Scrupe (or Scrob) who in 1067 was associated with the Castellans of Herefordshire in resisting Edric Silvaticus (who still continued to maintain the Saxon cause in the west) and that Richard's Castle derived its name from him as its founder. Auretone may, like Orleton in its immediate neighbourhood, have been simply a name given to the place from the abundance of orles or alder trees. Hugo Fitz-Osberne, the grandson of Richard, lived in the reign of Henry I and marrying Eustachia de Say, left her surname to his descendants, one of whom, Hugh de Say, who had been active in the Welsh wars and had the wardship of Norton Castle, Radnorshire, died about the year 1200 leaving an only daughter. She married Hugh de Ferrars, who thus became lord of Richard's Castle, an honour which the lady had two subsequent opportunities of conferring on her suitors. De Ferrers seems to have died about 1204, and his widow, Margaret de Say, still a child and possessed of great wealth, married some seven years afterwards Robert de Mortimer, a scion perhaps of the great house of Wigmore. He was high in favour with King John who granted him license to hold a market and fair at Richard's Castle. Four months after his death which occured in 1219 Margaret married her

Richard's Castle 1867

third husband William de Stutevill who enjoyed the barony *jure uxoris* and at his death in 1259 demised it to Hugh de Mortimer, his stepson. This baron was an active partisan of Henry III in his wars with the barons, being temporarily deprived of his Castle by them, and for his services at the battle of Evesham was granted the privilege of hunting the hare, fox, weasel and wild cat in any of the royal forests of Shropshire. He was sheriff of Shropshire 1 Edward I and dying two years afterwards was succeeded by his son Robert de Mortimer, Baron of Burford and Richard's Castle, who by his wife Joyce, daughter and heir of William la Zouch had two sons. The elder of these, Hugh de Mortimer had summons to Parliament in 1297 and took part in the Scottish wars. At his death his two daughters became his co-heirs and the Barony of Mortimer of Richard's Castle still remains in abeyance amongst their descendants.* *(Eyton's Salop, Dugdale's Baronage.)*

Joan de Mortimer, the elder co-heiress, had Richard's Castle and married, first, Thomas de Bickenore and afterwards Sir Richard Talbot who is said to have been a member of the Eccleswall line. By her second husband she had a son and heir Sir John Talbot, " of whom," says Blount, "and of his wife Juliana I have seen a deed in French, dated 23 Edw. III, wherein he writes himself Seigneur de Chastel Richart and it has a curious seal of armes. This Sir John had issue another Sir John † as appears by this Record " Johannes Talbot, miles, fil. et hæres Joh. Talbot de Castello Ricardi, militis, et Julianæ uxoris suæ tenet manerium Blatvagh et 10s. redditus in Lentwardyn in com. Salop de Rege in capite per servitium mediætatis Baroniæ de Burford, quondam Roberti de Mortimer." This last Sir John Talbot died without male issue (in 1375) and by his female issue the inheritance was divided between Sir Gwarin Archdeacon and Sir Matthew Gourney. After this the manor and rectory came, by what means

---

* The connection of these Mortimers with those of Wigmore is very obscure. Blount says he had seen a deed dated 1289 bearing the arms of the former, viz. " Gules 6 crosslets or between 2 bars wavy, wych without the crosslets were the armes of Saye."

† Proofs of Age. " John, son and heir of John Talbot was 21 years of age on the Feast Invention of Holy Cross, was born at Richard's Castle and baptised on aforesaid day and feast. A.D. 1337."

I know not,‡ to Sir Thomas Pope, Knt., and then to the Crown, whence by Henry VIII it was granted to Sir John Dudley and his heirs.§ Edward VI gave the manor of Richard's Castle to Nicholas, Bishop of Worcester and his heirs. In the last age Rowland Bradshaw, gent., possessed it by a long lease from the Bishop, and married a daughter of Arthur Solway, Esq., by whom he had twenty children, whose grandson sold the lease to Richard Solway, Esq., the present possessor (1675)." Richard Salway (son of Humphrey, a member of the Long Parliament) was a major in the parliamentary army and in 1654 ambassador from the Commonwealth to Constantinople. He served as M.P. for Worcestershire in 1653 and for Westmoreland in 1659. His facility in speaking made him much prized by his party, and though his attachment was never so great to the Protector as to the old republican principles, he was sent to the Tower at the Restoration. His descendants are still the chief proprietors in the parish of Richard's Castle and also the owners of Wigmore Abbey.

Leland describes the Castle in these terms, " It standeth on the toppe of a very rocky hill well wooded and at the west of the paroche church there ; the keep, the walls and the Towers of it stand but going to Ruyne. There is a poor house of Timber in the Castle Garth for a Farmer, it longeth now to the King. . . . There is a park impaled and well wooded but no deer." Since then the ruin has been completed and perhaps may have been hastened by the sharp engagement which took place in close proximity to the Castle in 1645 when a body of Royalists, 2000 strong, under the command of Sir Thomas Lunsford were surprised by Colonel Birch and routed with much slaughter. A few fragments of massive walls are all that now survive to attest the importance of this ancient border fortress.

‡ Leland says from the Lord Vaux.

§ Silas Taylor (*Harl. MS.* 6726) suggests that (Ambrose) Dudley, Earl of Warwick exchanged Richard's Castle for some other lands with the Bishop of Worcester. Ambrose Dudley was the eldest surviving son of the attainted Duke of Northumberland and the brother of Lady Jane Grey. He died s.p. in 1589. Among the Acts of Parliament 28 Hen. VIII (1536) is one concerning the assurance of the moiety of Riccard's Castle to John Onely and his heirs.

Snodhill 1848

Cowell's Anastatic Press, Ipswich

Snodhill Castle.

◆·●·◆

UPON the summit of a low but steep hill in the middle of the Golden Valley, and in close proximity to the site of Dorston Castle, may be seen the ruined tower of Snodhill,* interesting alike from its picturesque form and from the associations which have attached themselves to it. For more than two centuries it was the abode of the Chandos family, and though the hero of Poictiers cannot be claimed as a "worthy of Herefordshire," yet it is something that the county formed the cradle of his race.

The possessor of Snodhill at the Domesday Survey was a follower of the Conqueror, one Hugh l'Asne, whose quaint surname (like that of Lupus, Earl of Chester) may perhaps have been derived from some personal characteristic—the ass, it must be remembered, had not then fallen into his present disrepute but was regarded as the symbol of patient zeal. Roger de Chandos brother (not son, as Dugdale makes him) of Richard, the founder of Goldcliff, seems to have been the first of that family who held the honour of Snodhill. He died in the reign of Henry I, and sixth in descent from him was Roger de Chandos (son of Robert who went with King John to Ireland in 1210) whose name occurs in 1221 as

* Mr. Flavell Edmunds in his *Names of Places* derives the name from Snod, a variation of the Anglo-Saxon snœd, and signifying a piece of land separated from a manor. Snodhill, though within the parish of Peterchurch, is a distinct manor, or rather an honour to which several manors were dependent.

obtaining from Henry III license to hold a fair at Fownhope, within the honour of Snodhill (*Close Rolls*). He died about the year 1266 and was succeeded by his son Robert, who took part with King Edward I in his expedition into Wales. At his death, which happened in 1302, it was found that he held the manor of Snodhill by barony and the service of two knight's fees. His son and successor Roger de Chandos served in the Scottish wars *temp* Edward II, and received the honour of knighthood. In 1321 he was made sheriff of Herefordshire and in the first year of Edward III held that office and the governorship of Hereford Castle. To him succeeded Thomas de Chandos, whose heir was his brother Roger, the first of the family who was summoned to Parliament. He was cited as a Baron from 1337 to 1355 and had previously been made a Banneret by the king whom he attended in France. In Edward III he was constituted Governor of Hereford Castle, and previous to his death in 1355 granted the church of Wellington to Robert Foliot, the Bishop of Hereford. (*Harl. M.S., 6868.*) Neither his son Sir Thomas nor his grandson Sir John (who has been erroneously identified with his celebrated namesake the Knight of the Garter) had summons to Parliament, and the latter who held the Castle against Glendwr in 1403 dying without issue, 16 Dec., 1428, the estates in Herefordshire devolved to the surviving daughter of his sister Elizabeth (who had married Thomas Berkeley of Coberley, in Gloucestershire) viz. Margery, wife of Nicholas Mattesden, and to his great nephew, Giles Bruges, who, through failure of the other line, became the eventual heir.

Snodhill in the reign of Henry VI,* was the property of Richard Neville, "the stout Earl of Warwick" in right of his wife Anne, the heiress of the Beauchamps, and she, after the death of her husband, (who was slain at the battle of Barnet) settled the Castle and manor of Fownhope (part of the Honour) upon Henry VII and the heirs of his

* Richard de la Mere, Sheriff of Herefordshire in 1421, is returned as holding a moiety of the Castle and manor of Snodhill as well as Dorstone 14 Hen. VI. He was probably a descendant of Peter de la Mere, the first speaker of the House of Commons, whose family name is perpetuated in Tedstone *de la Mere*.

body. *(Blount's MS.)* Queen Elizabeth granted it to Sir Robert Dudley, K.G., the infamous Earl of Leicester, as part of the possessions called "Warwick's and Spencer's lands," *(Ibid.)* and after passing through the hands of the Vaughans, it was purchased from them about the year 1665 by William Prosser of London, *(Hill's MS.)* whose initials (with the above date) are carved upon the front of Snodhill Court—an interesting building constructed in great part of materials drawn from the ancient Castle. The manor and site continue in the possession of the Prosser family, the representation of which is now vested in the wives of the Rev. Thomas Powell and the Rev. J. W. Sawyer.

There seems good reason to believe that the Castle was erected before the close of the twelfth century for the keep tower, to judge from the scanty remains, is of Norman or semi-Norman construction, octagonal in form with buttresses at the angles. One of the gateways is tolerably perfect, showing an Edwardian archway and a portcullis groove, and there are still some fragments of the walls of the outer bailey. Within the Castle was a free chapel, certain portions of the tithes of which in Snodhill, Fownhope, &c., were granted by Queen Elizabeth to Cecily Pickering and her heirs. There are no traces of this building at present extant : in fact, the Castle, which was a ruin in Leland's time, suffered so severely from a bombardment by the Presbyterian army in the next century that it is even surprising that so much of the structure has survived. Either the head-quarters of the troops or the battery from which the numerous cannon-balls found within the ruins were projected was at a place called Scotland, about two miles higher up the valley.

The Castle key is in the possession of the Rev. T. W. Webb of Hardwick, and the bell was removed some 50 years ago, at which date there was a good deal of ancient armour in the Court. There are still some curiously carved corbels and massive oak beams to be seen there, relics of the stately Castle which have escaped its general ruin.

Stapleton Castle.

--◆-●-◆--

ALTHOUGH situated within the County of Hereford on its extreme north-western confines, the township forms a part of the parish of Presteign in Radnorshire. Blount tells us that it appears in Domesday under the name of Stepedune and was given by the Conqueror to Ralph de Mortimer, but it is evident that he misread Scepedune (*i.e.* Shobdon) for Stepedune, and it is far more probable that Stapleton, though not mentioned by name, was included in the grant to Osbern Fitz Richard. The first notice of it which we have is in a writ dated 30th June, 1207, when, owing to the minority and widowhood of Margaret de Say, it was at the disposal of King John; and Margaret de Say was, as we have already stated (*sub Richard's Castle*) the heiress of the Fitz Richards. One of her many suitors was Thomas de Galway, Earl of Athol, who, during the King's pleasure held both the Castles and, incurring some suspicion, had orders to surrender them to William de Cantilupe, but on the constable of Chester guaranteeing his good faith he was permitted to retain them. (*Eyton's Salop.*) In 1223 Henry III conceded a license to William de Stuteville, then Baron of Richard's Castle *jure uxoris*, to hold a weekly market at his manor of Stapleton until the King should come of age. The descent of the manor and Castle continued with the Mortimers of Richard's Castle and there is therefore no need to add anything to what has been stated under that head. At the death of Hugh de Mortimer, the last baron, in 1304 Stapleton fell to the share of his younger daughter and co-heiress, Margaret; she married Sir Geoffrey de Cornwall, whose father was a natural son of Richard Plantagenet, King

Stapleton 1850

157

of the Romans and Earl of Cornwall and Poitou, 2nd son of King John.   Sir
Geoffrey was the progenitor of the several branches of the Cornewall family,
one of which was raised to the Peerage in the person of Sir John Cornwall,
K.G., who, after marrying the Princess Elizabeth, sister of Henry IV,
and fighting gallantly at Agincourt, was created in 1433 Baron Fanhope
of Fanhope (or Fownhope) co. Hereford and again in 1442 Baron Milbroke.
From Sir Geoffrey's second son descend the Cornewalls of Burford * and
Berington and it is in the former branch that the possession of Stapleton Castle
continued.   These two lines can boast of many eminent members, and in
addition to those whom we have mentioned under Moccas, we must notice
the names of Sir Gilbert Cornewall who held Stapleton during the civil wars.
Charles Cornewall, of Berington, Vice-Admiral of the Fleet which defeated
the Spanish forces July 31st, 1718; his grandson Charles Wolfran Cornewall,
a Lord of the Treasury and twice Speaker of the House of Commons, and
his kinsman Foliot Cornewall, D.D. successively Bishop of Bristol, Hereford
and Worcester.

John Cornewall, Esq., son of Sir Gilbert, owned Stapleton in 1675
but it was sold in the year 1706 by Thomas Cornewall, Baron of Burford
to Auditor Harley, of Eywood, son of Sir Edward Harley of Brampton
Brian, and formed part of Lord Oxford's estate until very recently.   It is
now the property of Francis Evelyn, Esq., whose father purchased it
of the late Earl.

We have no means of ascertaining the character of the ancient
building, fragments of which are embedded in the farm house which
occupies the Castle site.   The Castle itself in 1645 is described in Symonds's
Diary as "strong but because there was no water near it was pulled downe
by Ludlowe's Governor (Sir Mich. Woodhouse) least the enemy might
make use of it." (p. 203.)   He adds the significant word "defaced,"
from which we may gather that the work of demolition was complete.

* The magnificent series of monuments to the Cornewall family in Burford Church have
been elaborately restored under the superintendence of the Rector, the Rev. J. W. Joyce.
(See Gough's Sepulchral Monuments, II, 79; and Dingley's History from Marble, II, 291, &c.)

Sutton Castle.

It is interesting to know that the site of King Offa's Castle or palace, the traditionary scene of St. Ethelbert's murder, is established by a series of unimpeachable evidences. The name of Sutton Walls indicates in all probability the Roman entrenchment which formed the basis of the Mercian town. Giraldus Cambrensis, in his life of St. Ethelbert, mentions some ruins of a Castle which he saw there, and in the Liber Niger of Wigmore Abbey *(Cart. 18 : in Bibl. Harl.)* the following reference occurs :—" Walterus Aurifaber Rector Ecclie de Dorsintune concessit Roger' de Moneume terras in villa de Sutton que jacent *sub castro de Offaditch.*" Leland, early in the sixteenth century, observes the " notable ruines of some auncyent and great building, sumtyme the mansion of King Offa, at such time as Kenchestre stood or els Hereford was a begynning," and in the next century though the ruins had disappeared, the contour of the ground marked, even more clearly than it now does, the extent and position of the palace. *(Gough's Camden.)*

It is impossible to reconcile the romantic accounts of Ethelbert's murder given by the old chroniclers. That which has obtained most currency reminds one of the tragedy of Macbeth. Offa, King of Mercia, daring enough in battle but inapt for a crime which violated the laws of nature and hospitality, is represented as indignant at his wife's suggestion that more could be gained by slaying his neighbour Ethelbert than by marrying him to their daughter Elfrida. But her stronger will overpowers his scruples. The day before the marriage a feast is held in the palace at Sutton : the guests drink deeply and in the stillness of the night that followed—

> Kinge Alberte...... is slaine in fulle privy wise
> Within his bedde, afore that he could rise.

Offa immediately seized on the territory of the murdered king and having profited to the utmost by his treacherous deed paid a liberal penance in the foundation of St. Alban's Abbey and the enrichment of the Church at Hereford.

Sutton Walls is said by Mr. Duncumb to have continued the residence of the Mercian Kings until Egbert, King of Wessex, united all the principalities of the heptarchy into one kingdom, A.D. 827. Be that as it may, Sutton was granted by the Conqueror to Nigel, the physician, and after passing through the hands of the baronial family of Frene (*see Moccas*) was divided between the Walwyns and Lingens.

The present lord of the manor is Thomas Evans, Esq., of Moreton Court.

Tretire Castle.

———

To the careful scrutiny of that eminent antiquary the Rev. John Webb is due the discovery of the site of a Castle in the parish of Tretire where he was long resident rector. All that is now left is a large squarish mound on which several towers appear to have stood, divided from the neighbouring ground on two sides by a fosse. No masonry remains but foundations may still be traced and the internal courtyard is well defined. A tradition was current some forty years ago that a gold spur had been found on the site and at the same date could be seen the adit of a passage formed by hollowed trees which conveyed to the Castle a supply of water from a brook about a quarter of a mile higher up. In the 13th century Tretire formed part of the possessions of Fulk Fitzwarine, an eminent feudal baron (descended from the celebrated Guarine who won by his gallantry the fairest bride and the richest domain in the Welsh marches), and became the dowry of his daughter who married John Tregoz *(see Eaton Tregoz and Ewyas Harold)*. But his succession to it was disputed, for we find in 20 Edw. I that Walter de Huntley and the other heirs of Walter de Mucegros impleaded John Tregoz for the manor as having been the property of the said Walter. *(Cal. Geneal.)* What was the issue of the suit or at what period Tretire came into the hands of the Brydges family we have not ascertained.

Twyford Castle.

———◦•◦———

SILAS TAYLOR mentions that in the parish of Eardisland (or as he prefers to call it Aresland, *quasi* Arrowsland) " there is on the North side of ye churchyard an old moated hall wch they call the Castle," and that in the same parish " at Twyford some report ye seat of the Penebrugges or Pembridges to have been." * *(Harl. MSS. 6726, 6868.)* We find, however, among the gentlemen of Herefordshire who were knighted by Edward III in 1306 the name of one John de Twyford *(Ashmole's Garter, 38)* and it is more reasonable to suppose that he belonged to this place.

The mother of the great Sir John Chandos, K.G, was Isabel, daughter and co-heir of Sir Robert Twyford, and it was by his uncle Sir Edward Twyford that the gallant knight was defended and carried off when in the skirmish at Lussac bridge he fell, wounded to the death. Whether there was any connection between this John de Twyford and these later knights of the same name we are unable to say.—Twyford was part of the possessions of the Mortimer family.

See Pembridge Castle. In the parish of Pembridge " on the S. part of the Church was the mansion house where there are yet the remaines of a fortified keep or small castle." *(Harl. MS. 6726.)*

Urishay Castle.

◆•◉•◆

IN a wild and almost inaccessible part of the parish of Peterchurch and on the summit of a steep hill stands the modernised farm-house which still bears the ancient name of Urishay Castle. The moat and fosse without and a desecrated chapel within the present building, are yet visible, but whatever other fragments may have survived have been incorporated in the house—perhaps of Elizabethan date—which occupies the Castle site.

The name Urishay appears to signify the hay or enclosure (literally the place surrounded by a haigh or hedge) of Urry and we find the word written "Urryeshay" in the fourteenth century.* It was held partly under the Mortimers and partly of the honour of Snodhill by the De la Hays—a family of greater antiquity than eminence, which produced a Knight of the Shire in the reign of Henry V and has generally had a representative in the lists of County Magistracy from that period until now.

Although we have inserted Urishay in our work because it has always been designated a Castle, yet it seems to have differed in no respect from such places as Treago, Gillow, and others—dwelling houses made sufficiently defensible to hold out against the attacks of a lawless neighbourhood, and to shelter within their courtyards the stock belonging to the dependent demesne.

* In the Inq. p.m. of Roger Mortimer, Earl of March, in 1398, John de la Hay Urry is returned as holding Urreyeshay the fourth part of a knight's fee and of the value of 25s.

Urishay 1865

Weobley Castle.

———◦———

O N entering the quaint old town of Weobley from the south there may be seen upon the right hand some large grassy mounds, encircled by a wide ditch scantily supplied with water and overshadowed by trees of no inconsiderable magnitude. This is the site of Weobley Castle—a fortress which we know to have been in existence as early as the reign of Stephen and the foundation of which has been attributed to Roger de Lacy or to his brother Hugh, (the founder of Llanthony Abbey), before the close of the eleventh century. (*See Longtown.*)

In the wars between Stephen and the Empress Maud it changed hands more than once. Occupied on behalf of the latter in 1139 by Talbot who took the Castle of Hereford, it was seized in the following year by Stephen himself (*Gesta Reg. Steph. 61.69*), during his successful campaign in the west. We find the Castle next mentioned in connection with the rebellion of William de Braos, whose daughter Margery had married Walter de Lacy, its then lord. De Braos had provoked the anger of King John, not more by his numerous acts of violence than by his just resistance to the arbitrary demands of the king, but he found it expedient to retire from his own country on the advance of the royal troops, and made use of his son-in-law's Castle as a fresh centre of action, issuing thence, in conjunction with Matthew de Gamage, lord of Dilwyn, to ravage and burn the town of Leominster. (*Price's Leominster, 14: Camden's Britannia.*) The date of this occurrence (which is variously narrated by the chroniclers) seems to have been 1208 or 1209. Upon the death of Walter de Lacy in 1241 the Castle of Weobley fell to the share of his younger grand-daughter Margery who married John de Verdon * and eventually descended to Margery de Verdon, the co-heiress of the second Baron. *(See Longtown.)* She was thrice married. Her first husband was Marcus or William Hussee by whom she had no issue: She then *(2 Edw. III)* married William le Blount † who was summoned to Parliament as a Baron from 1330 to 1337 and after his death bestowed her hand and fortune on Sir John Crophull, ‡ who in 1361 is styled *Seigneur* of the Castle of Weobley. He died in 1383, surviving his son Thomas Crophull who had married Sibilla daughter of Sir John Delabere and left a daughter Agnes, who thus became the sole eventual heiress of Weobley. Agnes de Crophull, a year after her grandfather's death and while still under age, married Sir Walter Devereux who in 1386 had livery of her lands on making proof of her majority.

Their grandson of the same name added to the estates of the Devereux family in this part of the county by his marriage with Elizabeth Merbury § and there seems good reason to believe with Mr. J. G. Nichols that these are the personages whose beautiful alabaster effigies are still to be seen in Weobley Church. *(See Notes on Weobley in Cambr. Arch.: Journal, 1869, by Rev. H. W. Phillott.)*

* Theobald de Verdon, the grandson of John, signed the celebrated letter of the Barons to Boniface VIII as " Dominus de Webbeley."

† Fines, 7 Edw. III, 35. William le Blount, and Margaret, his wife, and Nicholas de Colshull, chaplain, deforciant of the Castle and manor of Webbeley, &c., to have and to hold to said William and Margaret and their heirs of the king by the services due, and failing issue, then to the right heirs of Margaret.

‡ Her grandfather John Merbury of Lyonshall, keeper of the jewels to Henry V, &c., had married in her widowhood, Agnes de Crophull, *(Inq. p.m. 14 Hen. VI. Agnes quæ fuit uxor Joh. Merbury arm. desseisita de Webbeley Castro.)* His first wife was Alicia, daughter and heir of Sir John Pembridge and widow of Oldcastle. *(Hill's MS.)* Mr. J. G. Nichols considers it probable that the single effigy in Weobley Church, represents this John Merbury, but, as Mr. Phillott observes, the shield which formerly was suspended above this figure bore the arms of Devereux.

§ Fines, 31 Edw. III. between John de Crophull, chivaler, and Margaret, his wife, plaintiffs, and Ralph de Crophull, parson of the church of Cotyngham, deforciant of the manor of Webbeleye, &c., and of three knights' fees in Straddle, Kuesope, and Little Marcle, to have and to hold of the King to the said John and Margaret for ever.

Walter Devereux "appears for a time to have suffered for his adherence to Edward IV, for in 1460 we find him petitioning for pardon as a rebel : and in particular for his conduct at the battle of Ludford ; and in the same year a grant was made to Humphrey, Duke of Buckingham of fines due from him." *(Ibid.)*

His eldest son and successor, another Walter Devereux, espoused when little more than eleven years old the heiress of Lord Ferrers of Charttey, and acquired not only her father's title but the honour of the Garter. He fell fighting on the side of Richard III at the battle of Bosworth Field, having shewn two years before his death timely hospitality at Weobley to his ill-fated kinsman, Henry Stafford, Duke of Buckingham. *(See Kinnersley.)*

John Devereux, his son, married Cecily Bourcher of the Blood Royal, and in 1549, as a reward for his services at Boulogne, his successor was created Viscount Hereford, a dignity which has descended through his younger son to the present head of the family. His eldest son died in his father's life-time, leaving as his heir Walter Devereux who in 1572 was created Earl of Essex. He won high favour with Queen Elizabeth by his success against the insurgents of the North, by his graceful bearing and true chivalry, but lost it all in that grave of broken hearts, —Ireland—the land which seems to have had a malignant influence on the fortunes of his house. His sensitive nature gave way beneath the wound which his honour had received ; he fell a victim to dysentery and died in 1576, not without suspicion that the agonies of his premature death had been aggravated by the poison of his rival, Leicester. His son, the second Earl, was born at Netherwood, in the parish of Thornbury, which more than two centuries before had given birth to Roger Mortimer, Earl of March. There is faint parallelism between the lives of the two Earls ; a marked one between their deaths. Both were royal favourites, and met with the usual fate of favourites—a violent end. But there the parallelism ceases. Mortimer was simply an ambitious noble, unscrupulous and oppressive, who made the guilty love of Queen Isabella a means towards his own aggrandizement. Devereux was not indeed without ambition, but his ends were neither mean nor selfish. He was a patriot, a scholar, a poet, generous even to prodigality, full of sympathy for others and like his father, keenly alive to unmerited obloquy. That his love for his royal mistress was sincere we have no more doubt than we have of the sincerity of her remorse at his death. Robert, the third and last Earl, was not the least eminent of the Parliamentary Generals, and had he lived might have brought the quarrel between King and Commons to a happier issue. He fought well at Edge Hill and Reading and his services were not forgotten when at his funeral in 1646, the preacher expressed a wish that the bones of the Great Protector might be laid beside those of him who had been so able a lieutenant. By his death without issue the title of Earl of Essex became extinct and the manor and Castle of Weobley descended to his eldest daughter Frances, Duchess of Somerset. She died in 1674 and by a codicil to her will bequeathed her property to Thomas Thynne, afterwards Viscount Weymouth, who had married Lady Frances Finch, daughter of the second Earl of Winchelsea, the husband of the Duchess's daughter Mary. The manor and Castle are still the property of their descendant, the Marquis of Bath, and until the disfranchisement of the borough one or more members of the Thynne family always sat in Parliament as the representatives of Weobley.

Whitney Castle.

◆•◆•◆

We are unwillingly compelled to imitate the Danish writer on the Natural History of Iceland whose Chapter on Snakes Dr. Johnson was able to quote because it consisted only of the words " There are no snakes in the whole island." Of Whitney Castle we can say little more than that there is no trace of a castle there now, but tradition asserts that beneath the river, which changed its course in the year 1730, are still to be seen masses of masonry which might have belonged to such a structure. Certain it is that as late as 1675 the tower of a castle was, if not in existence, at least in the memory of those who had dwelt beside it. *(Blount's MS.)* No less certain is it that the place was the seat of a most ancient family which derived its name from it and flourished for some 500 years, yielding in nearly every generation one or more members of eminence.

The Whitneys, like the Lingens, trace their descent from Turstin the Fleming who held both Pencomb and Whitney, and being the mesne lords of both places took their surname from the latter. Eustachius de Whitney had a grant of free warren in Whitney in the year 1283 *(Rot. Turr. 12 Edw. I)* and in 1306 was knighted.

> " From him descended cross-legg'd knights,
> Fam'd for their faith and warlike fights
> Against the bloody cannibal,
> Whom they destroyed both great and small.

and they could point to their arms—(azure a cross checky, or and sable)
as a proof, which Hudibras did not possess, of the part they had taken in
the Holy Wars.   Robert Whitney was Sheriff of the county in 1377 and
like his father Eustace and more than one of his descendants, was also
Knight of the Shire.   The family intermarried with the Audleys, Baskervilles,
Vaughans, Lucys of Charlecote, and other well-known stocks, but the fate of
the main line was no uncommon one.   Sir Robert Whitney, its representative
at the time of the civil war, was a devoted royalist and sacrificed much
of his property in the service of the king.   Symonds says that his estate
was worth £1000 a year, but before his death in 1653 the valuable lands
in Pencomb had been sold and, by the decease of his only son without
issue, the name became extinct and the family property divided amongst
his daughters and co-heirs.   One of these, Anne, the wife of Thomas
Rodd, of Moreton Jeffreys, appears to have purchased her sister's shares,
but as her only son, Robert Rodd, of Foxley, died also without male
issue (in 1681) the estate of Whitney devolved on his second daughter,
Ann Sophia, who married William Wardour, Clerk of Appeals.   His
two sons, William Wardour, M.P. and Col. Tomkyns Wardour (of kin to
the ancient family of Tomkyns of Monnington and Garnstone) successively
enjoyed it and by the latter it was bequeathed to his godson Tomkyns
Dew, the grandfather of the present proprietor.

Wigmore

Wigmore 1844

Wigmore Castle.

We must confine ourselves as strictly as possible to the bare narrative of the History of Wigmore Castle, for it would require an entire volume to detail the fortunes of the house of Mortimer and to show the influence which successive members of it exerted upon the affairs of the kingdom. It is natural that a good deal of romance and fable should have attached themselves to the origin of so illustrious a family, and though no doubt there is a substratum of truth in the flattering stories of the old chroniclers, we think it preferable to follow the sober leading of Mr. Eyton, the accurate historian of Shropshire, in the sketch we propose to give.

"The annalist of the Mortimers tells us how Ralph de Mortimer * was sent by King William the Conqueror against Edric, 'Earl of Salop,' and Lord of Wigmore and Melenyth—how, after long siege of Wigmore Castle, Mortimer gained possession of both the person and estates of his opponent,— how he led him in bonds to the king to be consigned to perpetual imprisonment,—how lastly Mortimer proceeded to fortify the Castle of Dynethe in Melenyth which Edric had built." But Mr. Eyton regards it as

---

* Ralph de Mortimer is presumed to have been the son of Roger de Mortimer, the Conqueror's kinsman. He fought at Hastings and is quaintly characterized by a chronicler as "Radulphus de Mortuo Mari, omnium strenuissimus, velut alter Samson cum leonina ferocitate."

all but certain from Domesday * that Wigmore as an estate had never belonged to Edric Silvaticus, and that as a Castle it was neither built or even held for a day by Edric or any other Saxon. It was in fact the work of Earl William Fitzosbern who built it on "waste land called Merestun which belonged to Gunneret in King Edward's time," and the general conclusion at which Mr. Eyton arrives is that between 1072 and 1085 Edric Silvaticus forsook his allegiance to King William ; that William Fitzosbern, Earl of Hereford, being dead, Mortimer was deputed by the king to reduce Edric ; succeeded in so doing and was rewarded with many of the estates of Edric, but that he became Lord of Wigmore as the king's principal lieutenant in Herefordshire, after the forfeiture of Earl Roger de Britolio in 1074.

Ralph de Mortimer left two or three sons † and was succeeded at Wigmore by Hugh, the eldest, who opposed the accession of Henry II and fortified his Castles of Wigmore, Cleobury, and Bridgnorth (Brugge) in opposition to the king's order. Henry compelled him by force of arms to submit, and 1158 the Castle of Wigmore was surrendered to the king, but spared from destruction on account of its useful position on the Welsh frontier. This Ralph finished the foundation of Wigmore Abbey which his father had begun and died a canon of that house in 1188. Four generations later we find Roger de Mortimer among the staunchest adherents of Henry III in the baronial wars. " It was, probably, he who raised the exterior wall or at any rate made some of the additions to the Castle of Wigmore," (Sir Samuel Meyrick's Historical Memoranda in the " Analyst," vol. iv), and thither conveyed Prince Edward whom, in conjunction with one of the Crofts, he had rescued from imprisonment in Hereford Castle. (See Hereford.) The prince's gratitude was evinced, after his succession, by a

---

* The Domesday entry is as follows:—" Radulphus de Mortimer tent. Castellu' WIGEMORE Wills comes fecit illud in Wasta tra que vocat' Merestun qua' teneb' Gunnert T. R. E." We incline to think that the derivation of Wigmore from Wicenga (inhabitants) and Mere (marsh), agreeing as it does with the ancient appellation of the place, Merestun, (marsh-town), is more probable than that which refers it to the moor of the Vikings or Pirates.

† viz. William, Lord of Chelmersh and Netherby, and, according to some authorities, Robert, ancestor of the Mortimers of Richard's Castle.

grant of special privileges within the lordship of Wigmore, including the power of life and death. Simon de Montfort, robbed of his illustrious captive, revenged himself by ravaging the possessions of Mortimer, and it was not until the decisive battle of Evesham, where the lord of Wigmore commanded the third division of the royal army, that the power of the barons was broken. His services on that day were rewarded by a grant of the forfeited earldom of Oxford and numerous gifts of land. By his grandson of the same name the fortunes of the house of Mortimer were carried to their highest pitch. He was first summoned to Parliament in 1306 and though his career suffered a temporary check at its outset by the forfeiture of his lands on the charge of having quitted the service of Edward I in Scotland, yet on the accession of Edw. II he was at once restored to favour and constituted the king's lieutenant and justice in Wales, having all the castles of the principality committed to his charge.* The fatal influence which he subsequently acquired over Isabella, the wife of the weak King Edward II, is a matter of history nor shall we pretend to assign the precise measure of guilt which attaches to him in respect of the murder of the outraged husband. That bloody act vested the real power in Queen Isabella, and her paramour, for the young king could at first take no active part in public affairs, and Mortimer, having now no check, gave the reins to his insolent ambition and thus inspired with a common hatred towards himself the many foes whom private animosities had hitherto kept asunder. His own son called him the " King of Folly" and he was not long in testing the insecurity of such a throne. He was seized in the Castle of Nottingham,

---

* After the disasters at Pontefract and Boroughbridge in 1322, Roger Mortimer, lord of Wigmore was committed to the tower whence he had the good fortune to escape to France and enter the service of Charles de Valois. The lands and castles of the insurgents were seized and from the official surveys then made we are enabled to form an idea of the contents of Wigmore at this time. Alan de Cherletone, the custodian, makes a curious return dated 15 Edward II of the various weapons of war in the Castle. There were three Spryngholds, or machines for casting great stones or metal quarrels; crossbows of horn and wood, some fitted with stirrup irons for the purpose of winding up the bows, others of simple construction ; helmets for jousts and for real war, lances and spears, six tents and pavilions, suits of armour and coats of mail, the Irish axe (sperth de Hibernia), Saracenic bows and arrows, &c., &c. The effects comprised also a large chess board, painted and gilt and the *familia* of chessmen, a board for tables and draughts ; and in the courtyard five peacocks and good store of grain and beasts. (*Acts of Contrariant's Lands.*)

conveyed to London, and hanged at Tyburn in 1330. His body was afterwards interred in Grey Friars and is supposed to have found its final resting place at Wigmore. (*See Mortimer's Castle.*) By his attainder all his honours—including the earldom of March which he had obtained in 1328—became forfeited. His grandson, however, procured their restoration, and not only obtained a fresh grant of Wigmore (through the influence of his step-father, William Bohun, Earl of Northampton), but was also created a Knight of the Garter and appointed Warden of the Cinque Ports and Constable of Dover Castle. He died at Roveray in Burgundy 26 Feb., 1360, while in command of the forces there, and his remains, having been brought to England, were interred at Wigmore. He left an only son, Edmund, who became the third Earl of March, and intermarried with the lady Philippa Plantagenet, daughter and sole heir of Lionel of Antwerp, Duke of Clarence. In his will, dated 1 May, 1380, he desired to be buried in the Church of the Abbey of Wigmore on the left of the high altar, and bequeathed to the said abbey "a large cross of gold set with stones, with a relique of the cross of our Lord, a bone of St. Richard the Confessor, Bishop of Chichester, and the finger of St. Thomas de Cantelowe, Bishop of Hereford." His son Roger, born at Usk, 11 April, 1374, and baptised the following Sunday by William Courtney, Bishop of Hereford, was, in right of his mother, declared by Parliament heir presumptive to the crown, failing issue of King Richard II. He was slain in 1398 while acting as Deputy in Ireland, where his princely revenues seem to have induced in him a luxurious life unsuited to the savage natures with which he had to cope. His limbs, which Froissart says had been torn from him, were gathered together and transmitted to Wigmore for burial. Edmund, 5th Earl of March, was his heir and being but six years of age at his father's death,* was committed by Henry IV to the care of his son Henry, Prince of Wales. To the Yorkist party he was an object, as well as a pretext, for continual conspiracies and Lady de Spenser contrived

---

* Walsingham and other writers have represented Edmund Earl of March to have been taken prisoner by Owen Glendwr at the battle of Melenyth in 1402, while in fact he was at that time of tender age and in the king's custody. It was his uncle Sir Edmund Mortimer who opposed Glendwr and was captured by him and who, by Henry IV's neglect to pay his ransom, was subsequently converted into an adherent of the insurgent chieftain.

to steal him away from his custodian, but being captured before reaching Wigmore, he was consigned to stricter guard throughout Henry IV's reign. In later years he took part in the wars with France and on the death of Henry V, whose funeral he attended, was sent as Lieutenant to Ireland. He died, it is said of a broken heart, at Trim Castle in 1424 and, having no issue, the representation of the great family of Mortimer devolved on Richard Plantagenet, Duke of York, son of his sister Anne, Countess of Cambridge. With the struggles for the throne in which this ambitious peer engaged Wigmore Castle had little concern. On resigning the Deputyship of Ireland in 1451 he repaired thither and gathered round him some 4000 men to guard his progress to London, and thither also he retired when his armed protest against Somerset had met with utter failure. His death in the bloody fight at Wakefield was avenged by his son Edward, who, collecting from Wigmoreland a little army of friends and dependents, defeated Owen Tudor and the Earl of Wiltshire, almost within sight of the ancestral Castle at a spot "where the piety of the Mortimers had reared a cross that bore their name."

The conqueror mounted the throne as King Edward IV and thus Wigmore Castle became again a Royal demesne. It seems to have continued in the crown for more than a century until Queen Elizabeth, at the instance of Robert Earl of Essex, granted it to Captain Gelly Meyrick and Henry Lyndley, Esq., his stewards. Meyrick had shared the fortunes of war with his patron and subsequently, at the taking of Cadiz, received the honour of knighthood, but being implicated in Essex's attempted rebellion, was executed at Tyburn and his property confiscated. Lyndley (then Sir Henry), obtained the other moiety of Wigmore and in 1601 conveyed the whole, including the Castle demesne and lands, to Thomas Harley of Brampton Bryan, Esq., for £2600.* Sir Robert Harley was born

---

* A survey of the Castle and Park of Wigmore was made 8 May, 26 Eliz. by which it appears that the "twoe bridges there leadinge from the Towne of Wigmore into the Parke and Castle being very much decayed noe carriage can passe with any burden on them into the Castle or Parke. The first bridge, as well as the foundacon as in the tymber above wholy to be puld downe .... the other bridge partley decayed in the one end as well as in the foundacons as above ... the houses, buildings, walls, and other edifices in the said Castle beinge very much ruinous and decayed will not without greate charges be repaired : signed Robert Berye, Supervisor." (*Lansdowne MS. ii.* 82.)

within the Castle walls, and these, dismantled by the Parliamentarians in 1643 but with their historic associations unimpaired, are still the property of Sir Robert's descendant, Lady Langdale.

The ruins of Wigmore Castle cover a considerable area, and their character may be well ascertained from the accompanying birds-eye view. The keep was in the ordinary Norman style, massive and square with a slightly projecting buttress-tower at each corner. Below it, and connected by a strong battlemented wall with towers at frequent intervals, were the apartments of the Castle, and at the bottom of the hill ran a second wall, defended by a wet-ditch which Leland calls "a brocket sometime almost dry." Sir Samuel Meyrick assigns the erection of this wall to the time of Henry III, but if, as is probable, it is coeval with the gateway, it is not earlier than the 14th century. The entrance gateway which was reached by means of a drawbridge, is on the south side of the Castle and is the most perfect part now remaining. In the right-tower access was gained by a newel staircase to the porter's room, from which the portcullis was worked. The rugged and precipitous nature of the ground on the western and northern sides was in itself a protection, but the process of dismantling which the fortress suffered in 1643 has destroyed most of its ancient features. Lady Brilliana Harley, in an unpublished letter written in that year, says, "some say that souldiers shall be sent into Wigmore, I have put a few into the Castell which I hope will keep it," but it appears that Col. Massie could not spare either men or ammunition sufficient for its regular defence, and therefore it was thought most prudent to dismantle it. A detachment of the royal army passed through Wigmore in the summer of 1645,* but the Grange with its milch kine and stores of sheep made Mr. Cockerham's house more agreeable quarters than the neighbouring Castle, which no doubt presented to the eyes of Sir M. Langdale as to those of Capt. Silas Taylor only "a melancholy dejected prospect of stately ruins."—a description not inapplicable to it at the present time.

* A correspondent of the *Weekly Account*, who signs himself T. H. (possibly Thomas Harley) and writes from "near Wigmore, August 13, 1645," gives the above account.

Wilton 1845

Cowells Anastatic Press Ipswich

186

Wilton 1840

Wilton Castle.

———✦———

UPON the right bank of the river Wye opposite to the town of Ross and almost hidden by overshadowing trees are the ivy-clad ruins of Wilton Castle,

> At present but of little worth,
> In former times it had its day.

According to Leland *(Coll. iii. 303)* it was built by King Stephen about the year 1141, but as the manor of Wilton had been granted by Henry I to Hugo de Longchamp to hold by service of two men-at-arms in the wars of Wales *(Blount's Tenures)*, it seems more probable that it was erected by that feudal lord. His descendant, Henry de Longchamp, paid scutage for one knight's fee in Wilton in the year 1200 and with his daughter Hawisia the Castle and manor of Wilton went in marriage to William, Lord Fitzhugh, whose heiress brought it in dower to Reginald de Grey, lord of the honour of Monmouth and a baron of Parliament.

Their descendant, Henry de Grey, 5th baron, was summoned to Parliament as "Henry Grey of Wilton" from 1377 to 1394 and was the ancestor of the noble family which enjoyed that title till the commencement of the 17th century. Its most distinguished member was Sir William Grey, 13th Baron, "the greatest soldier of the nobility" sometime Deputy of Calais and Governor of the Castle of Guisnes. After a gallant defence of that fortress against the French, he was compelled to surrender it and became, with all his officers, prisoners to the Duke of Guise. His ransom was fixed at 20,000 crowns to raise which much of the family property was sold, and Gilbert Talbot of Goodrich offered in 1576 to purchase Wilton for £6000. As he writes to his father—"besyde the benefyte thereof, he myghte be able to attende on his Lordshipe with a thousand tall followers, to follow his lordship's directions, if he shoulde have neede to commande him." *(Lodge's Illustrations.)* However the sale was not completed and Wilton continued with the De Greys until the reign of Elizabeth when it passed by a family arrangement to the Hon. Charles Brydges, cup bearer to King Philip, second son of Sir John Brydges, 1st Baron Chandos. He was Deputy-Lieutenant of the Tower to his father when the warrant came for executing the Princess Elizabeth, and his delay in obeying it was the means of saving her life. His eldest son Sir Giles Bridges was created a Baronet in 1627 and his successor seems to have given offence to both parties in the Civil War by holding aloof from active service with either. Silas Taylor's account of the burning of Wilton Castle, which must be taken as the version of a sturdy Parliamentarian, is as follows—

"Near to the bridge of Rosse foreine stood a very fayre sweet dwelling house of Sir John Bridges wch in ancient times was a castle, of wch were held several knights' fees in this county; wch now being upon mencion I shall make bold to insert something in the defence of this knight, whom the cavaliers unjustly slander with the brand of treachery. He was one yt meddled not with the royall quarrell at such time when Herefordshire was overflowne with that deluge, but it being a time wherein most gentlemen interested themselves on one side or another, he beeing unwilling to take his rest on his bed of ease while England and Ireland were in flames, betooke himself to quarrell in Ireland as not well understanding the difference in England. At his return out of Ireland his designe was recruits for his comand there and staying awhile at his house he found himself in great odium with those that by the late undeserving king were as undeservedly trusted wth the command of ye country, viz. Henry Lingen of Sutton Esq: and one Barnaby Scudamore, a man of noe fortune, intrusted with ye government of ye city of Hereford, who betwixt them ordered the burning of this house, formerly ye Castle of Wilton, wch savoured more of spleen and malice than of souldierlike designe, in regard ye place was very unlikely to have made a garrison (it being seated not in a castle-like but house-like building) unless they wd have been at ye cost and paines to pull downe the house and built it a castle; but however burned it they would and did: after he had like a gentleman in the field had an account with Mr. Lingen, he came into ye parliament's quarters, wch these malignants of Hereford know well enough where when he had been a good space he layd that souldierlike design to his great honoure and their vast and lasting disreputation who in the city pretended soe much of soldiers, yet were soe carelesse of seizing on ye guard at Bisters gate in ye habit of countrymen who were summoned in to breake the ice about ye walls, wch haply tooke effect : he was not in the town but without with a great force as an enemy to them and their wayes wch he continued to his dying day." (*Harl. MS.* 6868.)

Sir John Brydges died in 1651 and was buried at Peterstowe. His only son Sir James, succeeded to the Barony of Chandos and died in 1714 while the patent creating him Viscount Wilton and Earl of Carnarvon was in progress. His son—the " Timon" of Pope's Satire and the " Princely Chandos" of popular repute, received not only these honours but the higher titles of Marquis of Carnarvon and Duke of Chandos. In consequence of some pique with regard to his political influence in the county he disposed of all his Herefordshire property, and Wilton Castle was purchased by the trustees of Guy's Hospital about the year 1722 and is still held by that body.

The oldest portion of the existing remains is the south-west tower, but the castle was evidently remodelled in the 15th century and the windows which escaped destruction by fire during the Civil war clearly show that the building at that time partook rather of the character of a castellated mansion than of a military castle.

The title of Grey de Wilton was revived in 1784 when Sir Thomas Egerton, Bart., (whose ancestor Sir Rowland had married in 1617 Bridget, daughter of Thomas Grey, 15th Baron Grey de Wilton) was raised to the peerage as Baron Grey of Wilton Castle, and was further advanced, 26th June, 1801 to the dignities of Viscount Grey de Wilton and Earl of Wilton, with remainder to the younger sons of his only daughter, the wife of the first Marquis of Westminster. According to this limitation the Hon. Thomas Grosvenor, who assumed the name of Egerton, became Earl of Wilton and still enjoys that title.

APPENDICES.

◆•◆•◆

Almeley.---Appendix, I.

The connection of the Oldcastles with Almeley and its neighbourhood is sufficiently proved by the following references :—

Cal. Rot. Pat. 7 *Hen. VI.*   Pro Henrico de Oldecastell fil. et hær.   Johis de Oldecastell, militis, Domini de Cobham, de manerio de Almeley ac aliis terris &c., in qua continetur totus processus ac attinctura dicti Johis.

Ibid. 10 *Hen. VI.*   Pro eodem de eodem man. ac de diversis aliis terris et tenem' in com. Heref.

Ibid. 19 *Hen. VI.*   Rex conc. Walt Devereux in fœdo tres acras prati in Webbeley nuper Joh. Oldecastell mil. att.

The pedigree of Oldcastell of Oldcastell as given in the Heraldic Visitation of the county in 1589 is as follows :—

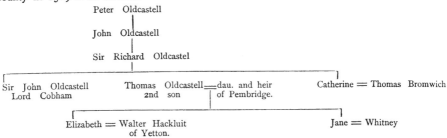

Peter Oldcastell

John Oldcastell

Sir Richard Oldcastel

Sir John Oldcastell Lord Cobham   Thomas Oldcastell══dau. and heir 2nd son | of Pembridge.   Catherine ══ Thomas Bromwich

Elizabeth ══ Walter Hackluit of Yetton.   Jane ══ Whitney

To this we may add on the authority of an old MS. in Dr. Coningsby's collections (*penes* Rev. A. Clive) that John Merbury of Webley esq. in 1418 held the manor of Eton (apparently in right of his wife Alice Pembridge) for life, with remainder to Richard Oldcastle son of the said Alice by her first husband, Thomas Oldcastell.

Among the issues of the Exchequer, 5 *Hen. IV.*, 27 *Feb.*, is a grant of £10 to John Merbury "for the good and grateful service by him bestowed and to be bestowed upon the Lord the King ; and also because that he married Alice Oldecastle of the county of Hereford."

Appendix II.—Bredwardine.

Charter 11.   Henry III, p. 2 & 3.

20 *Aug.* 2, *Henry III.*   King Henry III to the Abbot and Monks of S. Mary de Dora. Confirmation inter alia of the following grant :—

" De dono Radulfi de Bascarvilla tota' tra' desup' parcu' de Bredworthin scilt virgata' tre q fuit Nicholai Senescaldi et tota tra desup illam usqe ad fonte' Meredic sic servita vadit a tra q fuit Nicholai Senescaldi usqe ad fontem Meredic in bosco et plano, et ex alia pte de fonte Meredic usqe ad virgata' tre qua' habent ex dotacone ej' 'ex alia parte Vet'is Castelii q vadit usqe ad tra' Hug' Rustici sic divise et mete ipsor Monachor' fce et posite fuert cora ipso et legalibs hoibs suis et de tra p'dci Hugon' usqe ad rivulum q curret subt' t'ra que fuit Rogi filii Aalard usqe ad fossam parchi t p't hec duas acras prati, acram p'dci, scilt Nicholai Senescaldi et alt'am acram juxt ea' msura' msurata' et p' t' hoc totu' Benefeldu' ad pastura' oviu' suar' et pecor' suor.' "

Inquisitio post mortem Willielmi Fouleshurst.   18 Hen. VI, No. 11.

(Anno 1440.)

Inquis capt, apud Hereford in com. Hereford ultimo die Octobr anno regni Regis Henrici sexti post conquestum decimo nono coram Johe Aberhale Esc dni Regis in com Hereford ac March Wall eidem com' adjacent' virtute cujusdam bris dni Regis eidem Esc direct & huic inquis consul p sacrm Thome de la Hay Jun Thome Pembrugge Edi Gomond Thome Horsnet Willi Chamburleyn Thome ap Ithell Johis Croyne Johis Graunt Johis Bedyll Rici Pere Thome Watkyns Walt'i Bene Rici Broche & Rici Fletcher Jur qui dicunt qd Willus Fouleshurst in dco bri nominatus fuit sesitus in dnico suo ut de feodo die quo obijt de castro de Bradwardyn cum ptin & de manr'o de Weston cu ptin in dco com Hereford que quidem castrum & man'in cum ptin tenentr de dno Rege in capite p s'viciu quarte ptis unius feode militis.   Quia dicunt qd quidem Walt'us Baskervyle miles fuit sesit' in dnico suo ut de feodo de castro & de man'io p'dict in com p'dco & cepit in ux'em Elizabeth Lacy qui quidm Walt'us & Elizabeth huerunt exitu' int'eos Johem & Margaretam et postea p'dictus Walt'us obijt post cujus decessum p'dictus Johes in castro & man'io p'dict cu ptin intravit & obijt inde seit in dnico suo ut de feodo sine hered' de corpe suo post cujus mortem castrum & man'iu p'dict cum ptin descendebat p'dicte Margarete ut sorori & heredi p'dci Johis que quidem Margareta cepit in viru' quendam Robtum Fouleshurst & huerunt exit int' eos Thomam & postea p'dict Margareta obijt sesit' in dnico suo ut de feodo de castro & man'io p'dict cum ptin post cujus mortem castru & man'iu p'dict descendebat p'dco Thome ut filio & heredi p'dict Robti & Margarete qui quidem Thomas cepit in ux'em Evam filiam Hugonis Venables & huit exit Thomam & obijt seit de castro & man'iu p'dict cu ptin in dnico suo ut de feodo post cujus mortem castrum & man'iu p'dict cu ptin descendebat p'dco Thome filia Thome qui quidem Thome filius Thome cepit in ux'em Isabellam filiam Johis Bourlay et habiut exit' Johem & Willm in dco bri nominat' et p'dictus Thomas filius Thome obijt sesit in dnico ut de feodo de castro & man'io p'dict cu ptin post cujus mortem castrum & man'iu p'dict cu ptin descendebat p'dco Johi filio Thome ut filio & heredi p'dicti Thome filij Thome qui quidem Johis filius Thome obijt sesit in dnico ut de foedo de castro & man'io p'dict cu ptin sine exit de corpe suo exeunt post cujus mortem castrum & man'iu p'dict cu p'tin descendebat Willmo fratri p'dict Johis filij Thome filij Thome qui quidem Willms obijt sesit in dnico suo ut de feodo de castro & man'io p'dict cum ptin sine exitu de corpe suo exeunt.' Et dic' qd est in eodem *castr' quidam sit' qui nl val per annu' q vastat'*. et est in eodem man'io quidam sit' man'ij qui nl valet pannu quia vastatr. Ets unt in eodem man'o sex mesuag quor quolt dict sex mesuag valet p annu ulta repris. ijs et sunt ibm sex virgat terr arrabil quarz qualt virgat terre val p annu ultra repris vjs et sunt ibm xij acr prati quaru' qualt acr val p annu ulta repris xijd et sunt ibm sexaginta acr bosc quor quolt acr valet p annu ultra repris iiijd. Et sunt ibm viginti acr pastur quaru' qualt acr val p annu ultra repris xij. Et sic dimiss div's tenentibs ad voluntatem ibm solvend ad festa pasche & sci michis archi equis portionibs. Et ulterius dic dicti jur qd dictus Willms Fouleshurst nulla alia terr seu tent in dnico suo seu s'vicio de dco Rege nec de aliquo alio in com p'dco tenuit die obijt et dicunt qd idem Willius Fouleshurst obijt sextodecimo die mensis Octobr anno r.r. dci Regis decimo octavo. Et dicunt ult'ius qd Johes Baskervyle miles est consanguineus & heres ejus ppinquor videlicet filius Johis filij Rici filij Rici fratris dci dni Walt'i abavi p'dci Willi et est etatis triginta annor & amplius In cujus rei testimoniu dci jur huic Inquis sigilla sua apposuerunt dat die loco *&* anno sup'dict.

Common Roll. Easter 3. Ph & Mary role 410.

Hereford. John Vaughan Esq. *&* Milo Whitney gent. *versus* Watkin Vaughan Esq. & Joan his wife. The Manors of Cusoppe, Bradwardyn, Grove, Mochaas, & Allmaley * with app & 20 messuages 200ª of land 60ʳ of meadow 200ª of pasture 40ª of wood & 100ª of furze, & £5 of rent in Cusoppe Bradwardyn Dorsston Mockaas Allmaley Maddelay Kyngston Droxton (Thruxton) Kenchirche Kenerdisley & Letton.

John Mile *recorder.*

Letter of Watkyn Vaughan of Bredwardine to Lord Burghley, 17 *Dec.* 1584. *State Papers, Elizabeth. Vol.* 175, *No.* 35.

My dutie humblye used Good deare lord extracted out of our M'ches of Wales, comforte this bill tuchinge the co'enweale of her excellent Ma'tie obedyent and humble subjects in this m'ches For that we are enquered for murthers felonies in the next counteys adjoynant, viz. Heref. Shropshire, &c. by busie prosecut'rs by undue and ungodly meanes as at large appeth hereinclosed. Good L. beinge so chayned we are thrawlle and bound knowinge not when we shall have such a subjecte to make intercession, proceadinge of the intrailes of our m'ches, helpe us with the principalst bill or wth wch of both you thinke convenient, My daughter is maryed to

Sr. Harry Gate.† I have benne wth youe for service humblye and prostrate. O worthy Sicill and puissant peere, of stile, fame, and fatherely cheere. The princes subjects doe youe find indued with grace and noble mynd. I sent instructions for two bills to Mrs. Blanche,‡ Good my L. the one is profitable to bridle Papists. Thother tuchinge base captaynes, who make m'kett of the soudio'rs yt were convenient that one gentleman of ev'ie countie should be joyned wth the sayme, as at large appeth in the same instruccons, for if the gentleman did misuse them, yt would tutch his house and creaditt, Plackabilitie, curtessie, state and degree, wth sundrie rare vertuous peculier to thee. Thie style, lyne, worthye anncestors to unfold, unlearned, unskilfull in Genealogy to seme bold, The glorious highe and mightie & holie spirit powred upon thappostles defend youe my good L and yors wth a nomber of healthfull yeres, from Bredwardyn this xvij of Desember, 1584.

Your L. at comaundemt.
wth my service.

My hart doth pant, my hand
doth quyver, in Dutifull dutye,   WATKIN VAUGHAN.
your style to deliver.

    Pardon good deare L. for that it is in haste.

(Addressed) To the Right hon'able the L. Treasorer of England, yev these.

(Indorsed) 17 Decb. 1584.
(in Burleigh's hand) Watkn Vaugha.

---

    * This was probably a subdivision of the Manor of Almeley, and perhaps derived through the marriage of Whitney with Oldcastle. (See App. I. ante.)

    † Catharine, daughter of Watkyn Vaughan married first, James Boyle, of Hereford ; 2ndly, Sir H Gates, of Semer, co. Ebor, and 3rd, Robert Whyte, of Aldershott.

    ‡ Mrs. Blanch Parry, Maid of Honour to Queen Elizabeth. Her niece, Joan Parry married the writer.

Appendix III.—Castle Frome or Frome Castle.

The Grant from King John to Stephen de Ebroicis of the manor of Frome Herbert is printed in the *Fœdera*. The date of the document is July 26, 1205 and the duplicate in the possession of the Rev. W. Poole has the royal seal attached to it in a tolerably perfect state.

Among the Castle Frome title deeds is a grant from Richard II, " dilecto et fideli militi nro Simoni de Bureley subcamerario nro" of the manor of " Chastelfrome in com. Hereford cum omnibus pertinenciis de hereditate Elizabeth' Clodeshalle que fuit ux' Willi. Deuose Chivaler, quod valet perann. quadraginta marcas " The deed recites that the manor was forfeit to the crown because of the said Elizabeth's cognizance of the felony of William Devorouse. It is dated Westminster 26° June 10 a° reg. 1386 and has a beautiful seal appended to it.

Appendix IV.—Kinnersley.

Copy of an old Roll found in the Treasury at Thornebury Castle among the Evidences there. *Mensis Julii Anno XI*, 1575.

" In the second yeare of King Richard the thirde Duke Henrie of Buckingham came from Brecknoke to Webblie and with him brought my Ladie his wife, my Lord Stafforde, and my Lord Henrie and there tarried one week and send for the gentlemen of the countrie unto him and when he had spoken with them departed thens ; my Lorde his father made him a Fryse coat and at his departing he delivered his sonne and Heyre to Sir Richard Delabere Knight for to kepe until he sent for him by a token, viz. Et tu es Petrus et super hanc Petram. John Amgasse that went wth my L. away delivered my L. Stafforde in the little Park of Webblie to Richard Delabere Knight, and then came after Sir Wm. Knevet and Mistress Oliffe, and so they came to Kynardsley all together. And when they came to Kynardsley there were XX of my Lorde's servantes in the place. At that tyme Dame Elizabeth Delabere being servante to Sir Richard Delabere Knight tooke my Lorde Stafforde on her lappe and bare him amongst and through all into a chamber of the, place of Kynardsley, and then went again to get Sir Wm. Knyvet and the gentlemen and brought them into the Chambre to my Lorde Stafforde.

Or ever my L. of Buckinghame departed oute of Webblie, Brecknoke was robbed, and at owte the younger ladyes and gentlewomen and brought them to Sir Thomas Vaughan's place the Treatower, wh was Captaine of the saide robbinge wth Roger Vaughan of Talgarth his brother and Watkin Vaughan his brother and John Vaughan being feed with my L. everie yche on of them, and the least of them had Xli of fee of my Lorde wth other diverse Gent. which some byne alive and some bin dead.

A proclamacon came to Harrefforde for the saide Duke, his sonnes and Sr Wm. Knyvet, that whosoever would take them he should have for the said Duke fower thousand pounde, for my Lord Stafforde a thousand marks, for my Lord Henrie fyve hundred marks, the wch proclamacon Sir Wm. Knyvet redde himself and prayed tht hit should not misse but be proclaymed and then was theare greate serche made wheare the said companye was become.

And as all the gent: of Harreffordshire were sent for by Privy Seale to King Richard to Salsburie, and by that time Duke Henrie of Buckingham was brought by Sir James Fyler the thirde daie whean he was pitifull murdered by the said Kinge for raisinge power to bring in Kinge Henrie the Seventh.

And after the said Duke was taken the Vaughans made greate serche after my Lord of Stafforde and for the said Sr Wm. Knyvet wch my Lorde Stafforde and Sr Wm. Knyvet were in the keepinge of Dame Elizabeth Delaber and Wm. ap Symon.

In the meane tyme she shaved my Lorde Stafforde's bearde and put upon him a maiden's raiment and so conveyed him out of Kynnardley to Newchurch.* And then came Xopher Wellsborne from Sr James Fyler to Kynnardsley and said his Father commanded to have the said L: Stafforde delivered. And then answered the said Dame Elizabeth Delabere and Will. ap Symon that theare was none such Lorde there, and that shall ye well knowe for ye shall see the house serched. And then went he to Webblie to my Ladie and theare met with Sr John Hurlstone's brother and got my Ladie of Buckingham and brought her to the kinge to London. And the saide Dame Elizabeth and Will. ap Symon got the Lorde again to Kynnardsley and the said Sr Wm. Knyvet and brought them into the place of Kynnardsley and theare kept them untill David Glin Morgan came thither from Kinge Richarde and said Wm. Delabere was arrested, and said theare he should abide untill he delivered Lord Stafford, and then saide Dame Elizabeth and Wm. ap Symon that ye shall well knowe theare is none such heare, and ye shall come and see the place and hit please you, and so in great malisse he departed thens. The night beffore the said David Glin Morgan came to Kynnardsley the said Dame Elizabeth and William ap Symon conveyed my Lord of Stafforde and Sir Wm. Knyvet to a place called Adeley † in the Parish of Kynnardsley and there rested her fower days, and then the said Lord Stafforde and Sir Wm. Knyvet were got againe to Kynnardsley by

---

* Newchurch is a township in the north-east of the parish.

† Adeley, now Ayley, a small hamlet in the south part of the parish. There is a farm there called Old Castle which perhaps formed the mansion house of the Matthews family in the 17th century.

the said Dame Elizabeth and Will. ap Symon for because she could not convaye meete and drinke to them aright.   And she kept them theare one sennight, and then theare came a great companye out of Wales and then the said Dame Elizabeth tooke my Lord Stafforde in her lappe and went through a brooke with him into the Park of Kynnardsley, and theare sat with him fower hours until Wm. ap Symon came to her and told her how the matter was that noe man came nigh the place.   And in the meane tyme Sir Wm. Knyvet went out with one William Pantwall into the Feeldes and left mistress Oliffe in the place all this whyle after the saide Dame Elizabeth and Wm. ap Symon tooke the saide Lord Stafforde and went to Harreford in the midst of the daie, and he rydinge behynde Wm. ap Symon assyde upon a pillowe like a Gentlewoman ridde in Gentlewoman's apparell and I wisse he was the fairest Gentlewoman and the best that ever she hadden her daies or ever shall have whom she prayeth God dailie to preserve from his enemies and to send him good for time in grace. And then the saide Dame Elizabeth and Wm. ap Symon left my Lorde Stafforde in a widdowe house a friend of hers at Harrefforde and Mistress Oliffe with him and at that tyme Sir Wm. Knyvet departed from Lord Stafforde.

Lord of Webblie Walter Devereux Lord Ferrars fell on the side of Richard at Bosworth.

THE   END.

Index

To compile this index the book has been repaginated so as to make finding one's way around it easier, and greater detail added to the index itself. This added detail has created its own problems, for often the Rev. Robinson does not make it clear whether he his talking of two similarly named people at different times in the book or the same individual. Wherever possible we have differentiated between people of the same name, either by adding their maiden name, whom they married, place of origin or habitation, and/or title. In some cases this has not proven possible. Where this is the case you will find an entry under a family that reads, for example: John(s). This either means that more than one John is mentioned, with no particular individual details, or that it has proven impossible in limited time to differentiate with sufficient accuracy whether the John mentioned is the same over successive entries. In the case of the Mortimers we have added details to help clarify who is being referred to—not helped in the text by the Rev. Robinson allocating the title of 3rd Earl of March to both an Edmund and a Roger! We have also adhered to the spelling and abbreviations of names given by Rev. Robinson, including his variations as far as practical. With these qualifications, we hope this index is more useful than that in previous editions.

V500 M 80   B 20 DP 3   72908:1 P 1

CASTLES OF HEREFORDSHIRE

ISBN 1-873827-68-7